Hi Joshua!! J.

'03

J. P. PATCHES

∗ NORTHWEST ICON ∗

Julius Pierpont Patches
& Bryan Johnston

Bryan Johnston

**PEANUT BUTTER
PUBLISHING**

Seattle, Washington
Portland, Oregon
Denver, Colorado
Vancouver, B.C.
Scottsdale, Arizona
Minneapolis, Minnesota

Printed in Korea

"J.P. Patches was our
rock star."

– Steve Wilson
'Almost Live' Player

Before...

The Space Needle

Microsoft

Starbucks

The Super Sonics

The Seahawks

The Mariners

The Huskies won a Rose Bowl

The World's Fair

The Evergreen Point Floating Bridge

I-5 ran from Everett to Tacoma

The Kingdome

The 747

The last person leaving Seattle
turned out the lights

Bumbershoot

D.B. Cooper jumped

...There was J.P. Patches

A word from J.P. Patches

Whenever I pick up a book, the first page I read is the forward or the thank yous. Well, this is my thank yous!

I could dedicate this book to my immigrant parents who worked so hard over the years to give their three children a good education. Then again, how could I forget the wonderful broadcast people in radio and television who aided and guided me over the years. Or my family, who spent many a weekend without me because I was away putting in so many appearances. But I think this book really goes to you, the people who made J.P. Patches more than just a kid's program. You made me realize how important it was to do a show that was something the whole family could watch, and laugh at, and take away a smile to work or school.

So thanks, all you Patches Pals!!

...and now a word from our author

To fully appreciate how this book came about you have to turn back the clock a good fifteen years and have a healthy respect for serendipity, chance and good ol' fashioned dumb luck.

Right out of college, hungry for a chance to prove myself, but finding the television job market tough to crack, I gladly accepted a job at KIRO Television…in the cafeteria. But those months of stuffing napkin holders and making sandwiches proved valuable in ways I couldn't possibly have imagined at the time. One of the benefits of working the chow line is you get to interact with just about every person at the TV station. This is where I met Chris Wedes, the man I soon discovered to be J.P. Patches. He was still a couple of years short of retirement and I was a star struck kid who wanted to know everything that went on behind the scenes of the television show that raised me. He, and several Patches show alumni, were only happy to oblige. It seemed

707707070707

KIRO TELEVISION — 1530 QUEEN ANNE AVENUE NORTH — SEATTLE, WASHINGTON 98109

This is J. P. Patches . . . Talent Extraordinaire

Extraordinaire? Too Emphatic an adjective for J. P. Patches? Not at all!

J. P. Patches understands "the child" . . . . that's his life. Children believe in him and respond to what he says.

J. P. Patches consistently reaches more homes and more children than any other personality in the Puget Sound market.

J. P. Patches, with KIRO-TV over seven years, has built a reputation as "THE children's personality" . . . and he keeps progressing . . . into the confidence of the rapidly-increasing youth audience.

J. P. Patches has a morning and afternoon program daily . . . in addition to his Saturday morning show.

Color! J. P. Patches and his entertaining friends are seen on the daily afternoon show in color.

J. P. Patches brings a quick-paced zest to his shows through his zany friends: Professor Wiener Von Brown, space scientist; Gertrude, a "lovely" forever after J. P.'s heart and hand; and the unpredictable Grandpa and Grandma Patches.

Let J. P. Patches sell for you.

WRUL RADIO NEW YORK WORLDWIDE — KSL-AM/FM/TV — KID-AM/FM/TV — KBOI-AM/FM/TV

A sales "one sheet", used to lure advertisers.

like every day I learned something new about the Clown show, and the more I discovered the more precious the memories of the show became. It's like anything else in life: the more you know about something, the more you enjoy and appreciate it.

After finally getting offered an actual job in line with my broadcasting education, I abandoned my stint in the food service industry and said goodbye to the Patches clan. I played the inevitable game of TV station hopscotch, jumping from one town to another: Butte, Yakima, Portland, before coming back home to Seattle. It was here that J.P. Patches and I re-crossed our paths. I first saw him at a Greenwood Seafair Parade and marveled at the reaction that he still got, almost twenty years after he was last on the air. I reintroduced myself to him after the parade and, doubtful he would remember me, told him I used to serve him lunch about a decade earlier. We chatted for a few minutes and I figured that was that. Little did I know the wheels of fate were still in motion.

My twenty-year high school reunion was rolling around and I was coerced into helping with the reunion committee. During one of the meetings, following the requisite reunion committee beers, I was feeling a bit nostalgic and tossed out the idea of having J.P. show up at the reunion. A few phone calls, a few e-mails, and the Clown was pencilled in. I can still see it in my head, crystal clear, the moment I announced to my classmates on reunion night, "Direct from the city dump…"

I don't think anyone heard me announce J.P.'s name because before I could finish the introduction he waltzed into the room, and the cheers that erupted. . . I've heard quieter sonic booms. Eyes lit up, people were on their feet; I was thrilled to see so many of my friends had the same appreciation for J.P. as I did.

Months later I ran across Chris at Nordstrom and upon introducing him to my wife he promptly turned it into a vaudeville moment and made off with her purse. I looked at Chris's wife and said, "How long have you had to put up with this?" "Over forty years," she said, "I could write a book. Actually, *he* could write a book." The thought that one hadn't already been written amazed me. "Well, why don't you?" I asked him, but Chris just shook his head and waved off the idea. "Who would read it?"

Who would read it? Was he serious? I jumped in with both feet. "I would read it! And for that matter, let me write it!" But Chris wasn't interested. He said he'd been approached many times over the years about a J.P. book but he honestly didn't feel anyone would be that interested.

A couple of months later I was listening to a local radio station while driving into work and J.P. was on. It didn't take the Amazing Kreskin to figure out the radio station phone lines were lighting up. People were calling in with their memories and you could hear the joy in their voices. The minute I got to work I sent Chris an e-mail telling him that the radio program simply reinforced my belief that people are still interested in the Clown. Just for good measure I threw in that I would still like the opportunity to write the book. Imagine my surprise when I received an e-mail only an hour later with this simple response. "OK. CALL ME." I almost fell out of my chair. No, actually, I think I did, followed by jumping around the room, complete with tears of joy.

He still wasn't sold, but after a bit more arm-twisting he relented. I was officially given the honor of writing a book about one of the most popular and influential people in Seattle's history. I was also about to experience the old saying, in bright, fluorescent colors: *Be careful what you wish for*.

My wife and I were expecting our first baby. Not the best time for a husband to spend all of his evenings ignoring his wife, conducting countless interviews with complete strangers before sneaking off to the basement to pound away on the computer. Bless my beautiful wife and her infinite patience.

When I finished the manuscript and sent it off to the publisher, I was immediately consumed with tidal waves of doubt and second-guessing. What did I miss? Was there someone I didn't interview? One of my friends graciously cemented my fears when he offered up the type of comment that only friends can give, "I guess the eyes of Seattle are upon you." Great.

Writing the J.P. Patches book has been one of the most fun, rewarding, and memorable experiences I've had. Everyone I interviewed for the book was utterly gracious and supportive. It became very clear I wasn't the only person who held the Clown in high esteem.

J.P. Patches made a difference. A difference many of us in the Pacific Northwest will always hold dear.

Table of Contents

The View from Home..1

The Crew's View 5

From Kid to Clown: Chris Wedes: The man who would be Patches 9

Bob Newman: The man who was everyone else 27

What You Didn't See 41

Paying the Bills 61

The Sounds of the Show...67

More Than Just Props 71

How Big Was J.P.? 81

Characters..99

Theme Songs 105

Famous Guests 107

Other Notable Northwest Personalities 111

The View from Home

● ● ● ● ● ● ● ● ● ● ● ● ●

You turn the volume up on the TV so you can at least *hear* what the Clown is doing while you wolf down your Coco-Puffs in the kitchen. You push the bowl aside and race into the TV room just as Leroy Frump is dropping his ladder on J.P.'s foot. You laugh at the Borscht Belt jokes traded between J.P. and Miss Smith, as they play *Is it a hit* (ding) *or a miss?* (clunk). You secretly hope, with just the slightest twinge of guilt, that maybe, just this once, Miss Smith will win and J.P. will get the pie in the face. She doesn't, he doesn't, she does.

You fly to the bathroom during a commercial break and brush your teeth, like any good Patches Pal, returning just as Gertrude bursts in on J.P., knocking him to the floor. You hear Gertrude innocently ask what they call the support beams across the ceiling of gymnasiums and J.P. tells her that they must be "gym beams." You then hear your mom laugh behind you and wonder what is so funny.

A pint sized Patches Pal knows whose nose this is.

All kids got a royal reception from J.P.

You glance around, uneasily, as J.P. reads off names from the ICU2TV set, wondering if he really can see you through his magic television. You feel a little better knowing that at least you already changed out of your Winnie the Pooh pajamas.

You count down the days 'til you get to see J.P. in person at the new McDonald's restaurant. You stand in line with your best friend and your mom, wondering what you will say to the Clown when it comes your turn. You tell yourself you'll be cool as Captain Kirk, but silently hope you don't pee your pants. You flash back to the first time you met J.P., nine months earlier, when your troop actually got to be on the show. The line of kids magically disappears and you're standing before the rumpled hero-clown with the bright red nose and button covered jacket. All the blood in your body makes a beeline for your face and your ears grow hot enough to ignite wet grass. You hold out your trembling hand and timidly squeak that you were once on his show and wonder if he remembers you. At that moment, time stands still. You're vaguely aware of your best friend standing behind you, toeing the dirt, while your mom captures the moment with her Instamatic. The Clown's eyes crinkle into a smile as he bends down to you and whispers, "Of course I remember you!"

Your heart nearly leaps out of your chest. No prouder eight year old walks the earth.

You remember growing older, but J.P. never does. He is still there on your TV, every morning, regular as bran muffins and as welcome as spring.

Even in high school you occasionally find yourself not leaving for school until after the *Super Chicken* cartoon.

You remember reading in the paper that J.P. is being cancelled and you scramble for a pen and paper, flush with outrage. You practically burst with self-righteous indignation as you rip into the station for its shortsightedness and civic wrong-headedness. You vow never to watch channel 7 again. Two weeks later you're watching channel 7.

You remember enduring the patient smiles from your friends who didn't grow up here, as you try to explain why the name 'Ggoorrsstt' is so funny, especially if you live just southeast of Bremerton.

You remember going to a cocktail party, not knowing a soul, and wanting to leave as soon as possible. On your way to the door you notice a faded, dog-eared picture on the mantle of a disheveled clown with a little boy. You stop for a closer look. From over your shoulder, a voice, "I was nine. So excited, thought I was gonna throw up." You turn and meet the host. "Patches Pal?" you ask. Suddenly the two of you have a million things in common. Minutes later there are ten people standing around you trading stories. You stay until one in the morning.

These days you can't remember when you're supposed to make your mortgage payment or what time to pick the kids up from soccer, but you can still remember a worm named Sturdley, and a turkey named Tikey. It's funny how you remember the important stuff in life.

Griswald's bark was actually a German Shepherd's sped up from 33 to 45 rpms.

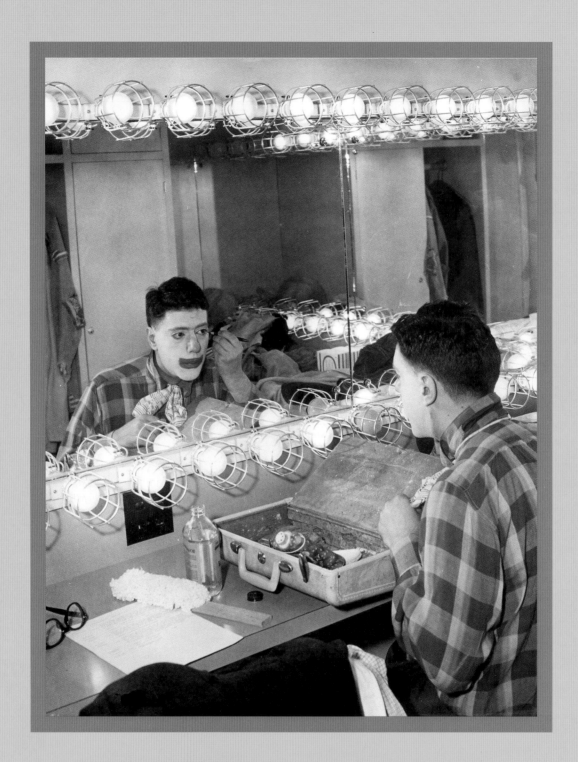

Average time to apply make-up: 15 minutes.

The Crew's View

• • • • • • • • • • • • •

To anyone who worked on the show he was simply referred to as *'the Clown'*. To this day that's still what they call him. For a crewmember, working on the Clown show meant looking forward to work every day; knowing that you got to start your day having fun, playing…and getting paid for it.

They got to see the man who was the Clown, Chris Wedes, disappear into a cramped dressing room, just an everyday Joe, a working stiff just like them, and come out twenty minutes later, a grease-painted icon whose talent could barely be contained within the studio. That talent: a rare combination of rapier wit and physical pliability. One part Jack Lemmon, two parts Ray Bolger, a pinch of Milton Berle, a dash of Sid Caesar — mix them together, pop it in the oven and out jumps J.P. Patches.

Twice a day, five days a week, plus Saturday mornings, grown men and women took their places around the set and played make-believe for an hour. You knew they were there, you could hear them — usually laughing. Northwest natives probably heard longtime Patches cameraman Roger Gilbert's laugh more than they heard their parents'.

For twenty-three years they watched the Clown and his two hundred-pound sidekick, dressed in drag, make prat-falls and wholesale silliness a daily staple for hundreds of thousands of kids, all the while slipping in jokes that no one born after the Roosevelt administration could get.

Throughout more than eleven thousand hours of unscripted zaniness the crew quietly waged a gleeful war with the Clown over who could get the better of whom. Water buckets and guile were their weapons, smiles were their victory spoils.

They had a front row seat for the creating of a Northwest institution, and most are convinced the Clown never quite understood or appreciated the impact he had on a generation of kids. When the Clown first went on the air TV was barely ten years old. You got three channels, maybe. There wasn't a lot of clutter. Viewing habits were different, attention spans longer. How popular was J.P. Patches? Ask a local native who the Mayor of Seattle was in 1968. After you get the blank stare ask them who was the Mayor of the city dump. If that was the final question on *Who Wants to be a Millionaire* every born and bred Seattleite could afford to live in Medina. Okay, maybe Eastgate.

The Clown's crew was a mix of men, women, old, young, Republican and Democrat. And no one seemed to notice. A dozen people; a single labor of love. No one wanted to disappoint the Clown. An impish Pied Piper leaving a trail of happy memories on both sides of the camera. A showman who always seemed to find one more laugh, somewhere inside his cartoon hat.

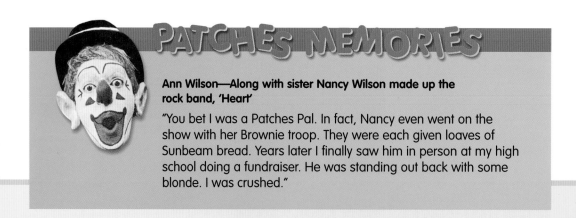

PATCHES MEMORIES

Ann Wilson—Along with sister Nancy Wilson made up the rock band, 'Heart'

"You bet I was a Patches Pal. In fact, Nancy even went on the show with her Brownie troop. They were each given loaves of Sunbeam bread. Years later I finally saw him in person at my high school doing a fundraiser. He was standing out back with some blonde. I was crushed."

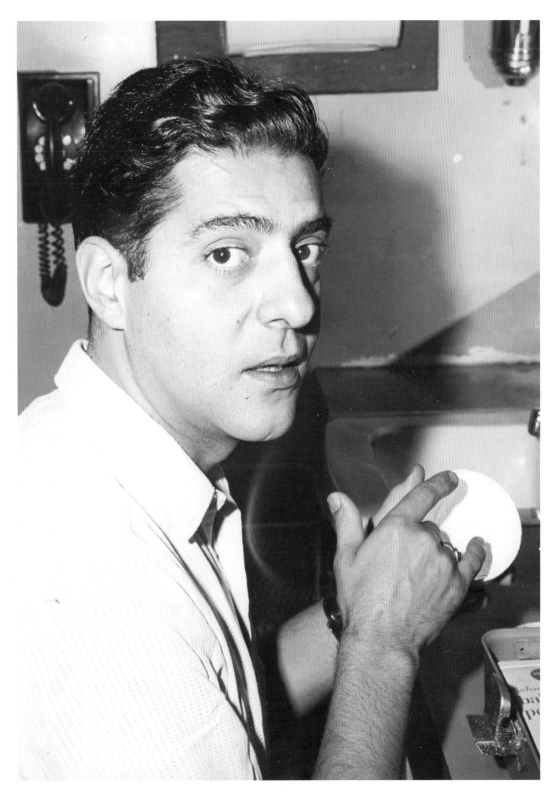

Getting ready to slather on the greasepaint.

A young Chris.
Almost looks respectable.

Almost.

Chris, the
college comic.

From Kid to Clown: Chris Wedes: The man who would be Patches

• • • • • • • • • • • • • • •

I should have known better than to ask a man who played a clown for a living what year he was born.

"I was born at a very young age," replies Chris Wedes, a.k.a., Julius Pierpont Patches, retired clown from the Ding-a-Ling Brother's Circus and Mayor of the city dump. It's always a bit surprising to discover that someone so completely ingrained in a city's history is actually not from that city. J.P. Patches and Seattle are like peanut butter and jam. You think one, you think the other. But the man who graced Northwest televisions for twenty-three years isn't from the Northwest, but from the North-*mid*-west. Born in Minneapolis, Minnesota, 1928, the second of three kids, Chris was raised in a family that had everything but money.

"We had literally nothing. We lived in what was called a cold water flat. It was an apartment over a bar with no heat," recalls Chris. "I still remember the rent, twelve dollars a month. Sometimes we didn't have the twelve dollars." Though growing up in the great depression, Chris says, they were still rich in the things that money can't buy. "There was no shortage of love in our house. It was the other stuff we were lacking. We had a single potbelly stove and my brother, Deno, and I used to walk down the railroad tracks and pick up coal that had fallen off the trains to fuel the stove."

Born to Greek immigrants who came to America expecting to find the streets paved with gold, Chris began earning his keep when he was only eight years old. He and Deno worked as paperboys. Since they bought the papers for a penny apiece and sold them for three, the boys felt like pint-sized Rockefellers. How many wartime jobs offered the potential to triple your investment? As a bonus, the owner of the paper had a weekly contest with the paperboys where he'd ask questions from articles in the paper. If you

PATCHES TRIVIA

Boris S.

Wart only

made one

public

appearance.

The kids

beat the

crap out

of him.

knew an answer he'd flip you a nickel. Chris took it upon himself to read the paper every day from front to back. He won a lot of nickels. That cover to cover reading habit is one Chris still enjoys to this day.

What's in a name?

Like most performers, Chris doesn't go by his given name. But the change had nothing to do with his television career; he did it just to simplify his life. Though it's Chris's last name that people still mispronounce (Wedes: pronounced *weed-us*, not *weeds*), it's his first name that he changed. It's not like he gave his name a complete face-lift, more like a nip and tuck. Chris's real name, in fine Greek fashion, is Christos, but he grew up answering to Christ (with a short 'i', like 'list'). After twenty years of signing his name *Christ* and having his teachers pronounce it like 'you-know-who', he figured it was time to drop the 't'.

Chris also had a nickname, given to him by his mother (consider this your first serious piece of Patches trivia). Chris's nickname was *Tikey*, which is derived from Greek grammar. In Greek, the diminutive addition to a name or word is *ikey*, so if a guy's name was *Basil*, his diminutive name would be *Basilikey*. Kind of like when we call little kids named *Bill*, *Billy*, or *Jim*, *Jimmy*. For the young Christ it was *Christikey*. Thus, *Tikey*. Thus, the name that twenty-five years later would become linked with a rubber chicken, masquerading as a turkey: *Tikey Turkey*.

A budding career

Chris was only four years old when he got his first taste of the limelight. He was part of a neighborhood production, playing the role of the sun. His job was pretty simple: hold a big gold paper disc in front of himself and walk onto the stage where all the other kids were playing the parts of flowers. It occurred to Chris that no one in the audience could see him behind the paper sun so he took it upon himself to stick his head out. It was the first time he'd heard laughter and applause directed at him. The seeds of showmanship were sown.

That showmanship came in handy a few years later when Chris got his

The drama! The passion! The chest hair!

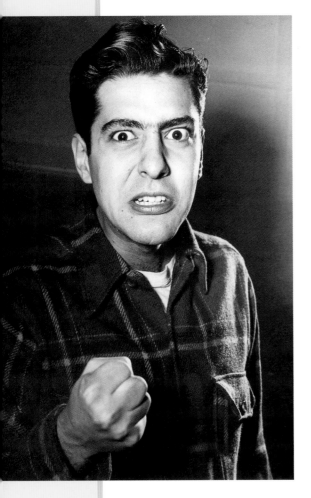

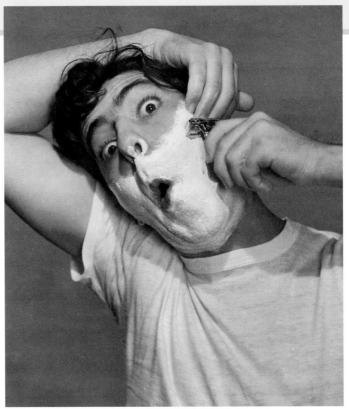

20 something Chris in a lather.

The power! The raw,
sexual energy!
The mono-brow!

first paying radio gig at the age of eleven. He'd been asked to play a paperboy for the *Catholic Digest* radio show, which dramatized stories from its magazine. After Chris did his brief bit, hollering, "Extra! Extra! Read all about it!" with all the verve and pathos of a young Olivier, the show's producer asked Chris how old he was. When Chris told him he was eleven the producer told him, "Then I'll pay you eleven dollars." Without missing a beat Chris responded, "I wish I was fifty."

School. Work.

Although Chris wasn't a bad student he quickly discovered good grades took hard work. A good laugh? Piece of cake. You guess which one he favored. This wouldn't have been a problem except Chris had the distinct disadvantage of following his older brother, Deno, through the hallowed halls of education. His annoyingly intelligent, straight arrow bother had the audacity to become the high school valedictorian, leaving a scholastically unmotivated Chris in his very wide wake. When Chris had the misfortune of taking a class that his brother had taken a few years earlier the teachers would look Chris over appraisingly and say, "Ooh, you're Deno's brother!" But then after a couple of weeks of witnessing Chris's class-clown antics the inflection would change to "You're Deno's brother?"

Getting an education was paramount in the Wedes household. Chris's grandfather had been a doctor so his mother knew the importance of going to school. According to Chris, everything his parents did was for the benefit of the kids. This family devotion was just one more facet to the huge influence his parents had on Chris's life. He got his sense of humor from his mother and his humility from his father. "My mother was a character," says Chris, "but a brilliant character. And my dad was salt-of-the-earth. The man didn't have an enemy in the world."

Chris had such respect and admiration for his parents that he couldn't bear the thought of disappointing them. He knew how hard they worked to put food on the table so Chris felt he should follow their example. Just going to school wasn't enough. Throughout his entire education Chris also brought home a paycheck. When he was fifteen he finished his hitch as a paperboy and began working at his dad's diner, *George's Coney Island*. It was a job he kept for many years to come. Through all of high school and most of college Chris's life followed a pretty consistent schedule: go to school, go to the diner, go home, go to bed, wake-up, repeat. When it was time for Chris to pick a college he chose Macalester College. "I really didn't know what I wanted to study," recalls Chris. "I wanted to go to the University but we lived in St. Paul at the time, and for me to go to the University, which was in Minneapolis, required two trolley tokens. Macalester College only required one."

PATCHES MEMORIES

Jim Zorn—Seahawks QB (1976-85)

"He was already a legend in Seattle when I got there in '76, but it didn't take long for me to get a sense of respect for J.P. because he always seemed to have a smile on his face. On the air, at public appearances, didn't matter, he was always upbeat and played it loose. That looseness, that playing for the moment is what set the show apart from other kid's shows. If a dog was man's best friend, J.P. was a kid's best friend."

Radio drama back when microphones looked cool.

In college he worked forty hours a week and still carried a full class load. Since it was during these years that he finally gave-in to the show biz bug, he managed to find time to perform in the occasional play, but outside of that his social life centered on pick up lines in the vein of, "You want crackers with that chili?"

Chris attended Macalester College from 1946-49. During that time, Chris performed his share of theatre (*Murder in the Cathedral, The Inspector General, Henry VIII, Julius Caesar*—Chris can still recite a lot of his lines on command) but also found another way to hone his improvisational skills. Chris and a few buddies started their own radio station, WBOM (Broadcasting Over Macalester). The station was only powerful enough to reach the edges of campus, but it was all the excuse they needed to act out their own dramas, comedies and any bit that came to mind. There were four of them goofing around on the radio. One of them, Roger Awsumb, describes how their careers went after college, "John (Gallos) became Clancy the Cop (local TV kid's show), I became Casey Jones (local TV kid's show), Chris became J.P. Patches (local TV kid's show), but we were never sure what ever happened to Fritz?" As in Mondale. Yes, *that* Fritz Mondale, alias, Walter Mondale, alias Vice President of the United States. "The guys used to really give me a bad time about the business I got into," recalls the former VP, "in fact they used to say,

'Hey, Fritz, isn't it funny how we all got into professions where people laugh at us?'"

Soon after college, through the help of his radio buddy, John Gallos, Chris landed a full-time gig at KYSM radio in Mankato, Minnesota. Chris worked as a DJ, read the news, and announced station breaks. But Chris's career in radio was about to take a slight detour, to Korea.

Next stop, Southeast Asia

When Chris was drafted in '52 and shipped overseas, a commander asked him what he did as a civilian. Chris told him he worked in radio. If

A lean, mean fighting machine.

The voice of Chief MoonRay, whom you never saw, only heard, was actually the recording of a Cherokee Indian reading the Bible.

Serving Uncle Sam.

you're thinking Chris spent his military hitch doing a Korean version of Robin Williams in *Good Morning, Viet Nam*, think again. After learning of Chris's radio experience the commander said, "Good, we need someone in radio,"…and sent him off to be a forward observer.

His job was to hunker down in a concrete bunker on the front lines, look for the enemy and radio back what he saw. It was usually pretty easy to spot the enemy. They were the ones shooting at him. But luck was on Chris's side. After only a few days Chris contracted a particularly nasty stomach virus that took off the hill. Two weeks later, before Chris could return, the bunker was overrun and the guys at his observation point were captured.

Goodbye radio, hello TV

After his two-year tour of duty, Chris came back to Minnesota and was quickly hired back at KYSM radio. While Chris had been away one of his college radio buddies, Roger Awsumb, had begun hosting a kid's show on a local TV station. It was called *Lunch with Casey*. Roger told Chris that they were looking for a floor director and that the job might also include some on-camera work. Chris didn't have any TV experience but with his theater background they supposed he might be able to figure it out. Chris officially had his foot in the door.

PATCHES MEMORIES

Sonny Sixkiller—Husky QB (1970-72)
"After playing in the World Football League I was back in town and Chris invited me to be on the show with him. I was so excited! I told my wife, 'Hey, I'm gonna be on the J.P. Patches show!' While I was on the show, J.P. asked me to throw a pass. When I cocked my arm, I said, 'I sure hope Jack Patera's watching.'"
(Patera was the Seahawks head coach)

Joe the Cook, and company

Lunch with Casey aired at noon and the daily schtick was that Casey Jones would pull his train into the roundhouse and go over to Joe the Cook's lunch counter. The only problem was there wasn't anyone playing Joe the Cook. So Chris donned a chef's hat, slapped on a mustache, bugged out his eyes and talked with his most extreme Greek accent. *Voila!* Joe the Cook! At that time many of the kids in the Twin Cities went home from school for lunch so *Lunch with Casey* had a huge audience. Almost instantly, Joe the Cook became so popular that he got his own show. There was another show

Joe with Roo-Roo the Kangaroo (Roger Awsumb).

The Lone Ranger, Roo-Roo the Kangaroo, The Whip, Joe the Cook.

on Saturdays called *Wrangler Steve* and he also needed a side-kick, so Chris pasted on a dusty beard and became the grizzled, old *Chuckwagon Chuck* ("Hey, Buckaroo Buddies, we've got a Jim-dandy, Hop-along-Cassidy movie today!"). Eventually Wrangler Steve left so Chris ended up taking over the show. Then there was another show called *Captain 11* (Todaaaay's man of the futurrrrre!) with a fella named Jim Lange (future host of the Dating Game) as the space man Captain. When Lange quit and headed for Hollywood Chris took over that role, too. So just to keep you up to speed, Chris was at one time *Joe the Cook, Chuckwagon Chuck,* and *Captain 11.*

The interview with the guy with the funny name

Even though he was now a full time TV guy, Chris didn't completely abandon his radio roots. Occasionally a friend would ask him to fill in on his DJ shift and Chris, not one to turn down a little extra cash, would sit in. It was during one of these gigs that Chris had an interesting, unexpected guest. It was a request-only radio show that ran from midnight to 8 a.m., and they only played requests that arrived by telegram. Since the telegrams cost eighty-three cents each, and the DJ got to keep fifty of those cents, Chris really played up

Tough Steak

Although he has not gained a world-wide name as a comedian, Chris Wedes, Macalester college senior, is doing well enough to earn part of his college expenses with a comedy act. He, too, has a problem similar to the better known laugh provokers. His stock routine is a comic waiter act which he puts on at parties and banquets. Doing this act time after time became tiresome to Chris so just for change, he decided to reverse the procedure and instead of playing the waiter be the diner. The result—Chris trying to eat a steak—makes an amusing study in pantomime.

St. Paul Paper 1949 Feb.

"A Steak this thick."   "Tools must be sharp."   Hot and delicious looking.   Choice section.

Dull knife?   Firm hold.   Perseverance   Anticipation

Leather is more tender.   Swallowing hard.   "Burp"   "Oh! Waiter"

A rubber-faced Chris with the 12 step steak program.

the request angle. Sometime after midnight Chris got a call from his wife, Joanie, who was working as the station's late night receptionist. She said she had someone in the lobby who wanted to come on the show for an interview. Chris wasn't expecting anyone so he asked who it was. Joanie said, "He says his name is Elvis Presley, and he's got some guy with him named…hold on, 'excuse me, what did you say your name was? Oh, okay…' Colonel Parker."

Chris vaguely recognized Elvis's name from a record he'd played earlier — something off Sun Records, *Blue Suede Shoes* — and told Joanie to send them up. Apparently Elvis and the Colonel were listening to the show in a cab, heading to their hotel, and figured it was a chance for some cheap publicity. Chris chatted with Elvis for about ten minutes, all the while thinking, "This guy is so shy and quiet he'll never make it in the music business." Six months later, Elvis became more popular than ice cream and Chris's future as a talent scout vaporized.

Station to station

While Chris's man-of-many-faces bit was going on at WMIN-TV, channel 11 in St. Paul, across the river in Minneapolis, another station, WTCN-TV was *also* airing on channel 11. How? WMIN would be on the air for two hours, then someone, somewhere, would throw a switch and WTCN would be on the air for two hours. Welcome to the wacky world of Stone Age television. Why the FCC ever let this go on is anyone's

Captain 11. Today's man of the future.

Minneapolis — Capt. Squint.

guess. Finally, someone came to their senses, bought the two stations and combined them into one. They chose to work out of the WTCN studios over in Minneapolis because it had newer, niftier gear. In other words, the equipment wasn't falling apart quite as much. Even before the merger, WTCN had its own gallery of kid's shows and its flagship show featured an amiable clown named J.P. Patches. When the stations came together they had a daily kid's show line up of *J.P. Patches* in the morning, *Lunch with Casey* at noon, then later in the afternoon it was *Captain 11*, *Skipper Darl*, *Joe the Cook*, and *Sheriff Sev*. Four kid's shows, back to back to back to back. And Chris was hosting two of them, not including his gig as *Chuckwagon Chuck* on Saturdays. And just for good measure, on *Skipper Darl* he played a whole slew of characters. Talk about job security.

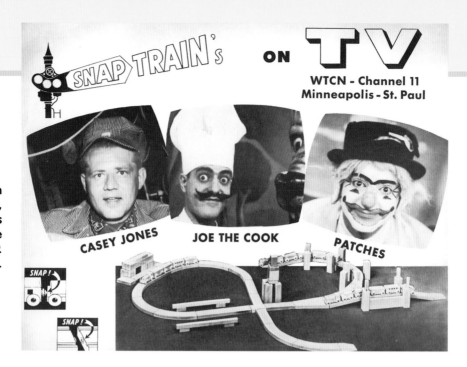

SNAP TRAIN's ON TV

WTCN - Channel 11
Minneapolis - St. Paul

CASEY JONES   JOE THE COOK   PATCHES

TV ad in Minneapolis, when Chris was Joe the Cook & J.P. Patches.

But I don't want to be a clown

A few months later the guy who was playing J.P. Patches took a job at another station in town and tried to take the character of J.P with him. WTCN owned the name and said no dice. He jumped ship anyway and came up with

1957 — J.P., before he lost the evil eyebrows.

another clown, named *T.N. Tatters.* J.P. Patches was suddenly in limbo and WTCN had some big clown shoes to fill. The station's program director, Fred Kaufman, turned to his trusty Chris-of-all-trades and asked him to answer the call of the clown.

"Actually, that's not quite true," recalls Chris. "He *told* me to do it." Chris said thanks, but no thanks. He didn't like the idea of slapping on all that grease paint every day. But Fred Kaufman was a persuasive man. Chris finally caved in, came up with a slightly different face for Patches (one that he eventually changed; too mean looking) and went on the air. The switchboard lit up! Angry parents flooded the station with calls telling them to take the new guy off the air, "He's not J.P. Patches!" But Chris's boss wouldn't let him give up. Within three months J.P. Patches was beating T.N. Tatters in the ratings.

• J.P. Patches •

Heading west

One year later, in 1958, Fred Kaufman came west to Seattle to help put a new station on the air, KIRO-TV. He called Chris and asked him to grab his grease paint and join him. So Chris packed up the family and headed for the strange new world of the Pacific Northwest, taking a pay cut for his troubles ($600/month, down from $800). On Feb 10th, 1958, a Monday morning, at 10 o'clock, The *J.P. Patches Show* went on the air on KIRO-TV, the station's first live broadcast.

Seattle's new personalities

Just like in Minneapolis, Chris was asked to carry more than one show. Along with the weekday morning Patches show, Chris also hosted another kiddy show called *Mystic Mountain*, which aired at 5 p.m. Years later he took on the responsibility of hosting yet another show on KIRO-TV, the short lived Saturday kid's show, *Andy and Sport*.

Ironically, it was *Mystic Mountain* not *J.P. Patches* that Chris was banking on to break through. On *Mystic*, Chris played the German accented, slightly Einstein looking Professor Friedelfurter (or as the kids called him, Professor Hot Dog, since they couldn't pro-

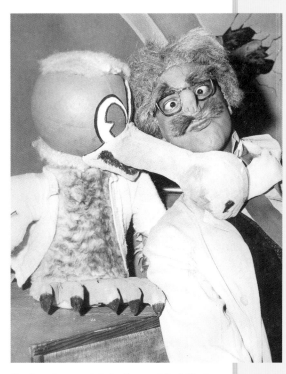

Be-Bop Buzzard & Professor Friedelfurter

PATCHES MEMORIES

Walter Mondale——Vice President of the United States under Jimmy Carter (1977-80)

"Years before he was ever on television I always thought Chris had an incredible entertainment talent. There was a group of us back in college who would hang out in my dorm room and Chris would do this skit where he would pretend he was his father translating the newspaper to his mother. He'd use that thick Greek accent of his and just butcher the translation, but he would look so earnest and acted like he had such complete mastery of the language that it just cracked us up. He had an amazing talent."

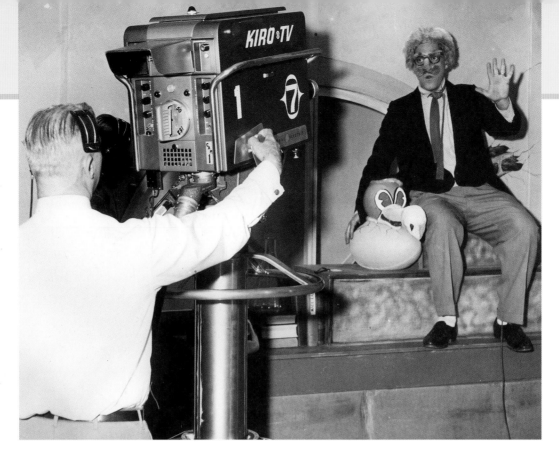

1958. Professor Friedelfurter with a freshly hatched Be-Bop Buzzard.

nounce Friedelfurter). The Professor's frequent guest was the jive talking Be-Bop Buzzard (voiced by Cy Flory, a director at the station). Together, the Professor and Be-Bop spent the majority of the time saving the earth from the evil Martian, Boris Blastoff (voiced by Dick Hawkins). Boris would show up in a little flying saucer, which slid down a piano wire to give it a spacey sound. The saucer would land on a table with a hole in it where a guy under the table would reach up through the saucer with a sock-puppet on his hand. Like any kid's show at the time, *Mystic Mountain* had a few cartoons sprinkled throughout the show, but the only laughs they generated were because of how terrible they were. Some of them were even silent cartoons, where they would just play music in the background so they wouldn't be so uncomfortably quiet. Chris remembers one cartoon in particular that didn't run on *Mystic Mountain*, but rather on the Patches show. It was called *Clutch Cargo*, and according to Chris, it was pretty lame. The cartoon wasn't even animated! It was just a series of stills with real mouths superimposed over the pictures to get the characters of Clutch Cargo, Spinner and Paddlefoot to talk.

Mystic Mountain was the show that Chris had such high hopes for, but sadly Professor Friedelfurter and company didn't last. After six months, KIRO's owner, Saul Haas, decided that J.P. should air in both the morning *and*

PATCHES TRIVIA

the afternoon, so *Mystic Mountain* was tossed by the wayside. Chris was terribly disappointed. He loved doing Professor Friedelfurter. He also knew that the professor was popular with the kids. During a fund-raiser at the Seattle Center, when all the kid show hosts were there (Stan Boreson, Captain Puget, Brakeman Bill, Wunda Wunda), Chris was backstage meeting them for the first time. Suddenly, from the mass of kids out front, a chant began to fill the air: "We want Hot Dog! We want Hot Dog!" Chris was stunned. At that point he'd only been on the air for a couple of months! Those cheers were a sign of things to come.

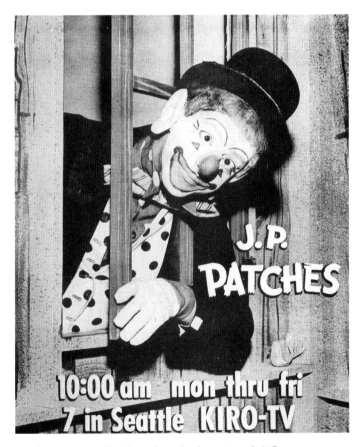

Yes, the show first aired at 10am, briefly.

They came up with the name for Chief MoonRay by reversing the name of then Seattle Police Chief Ramon.

• From Kid to Clown: Chris Wedes •

Bob Newman

SWF in search of J.P.P.

Bob Newman:
The man who was everyone else

● ● ● ● ● ● ● ● ● ● ● ● ● ●

In 1960, a 6'2", lantern-jawed ex-marine was hired by KIRO as a weekend film editor and floor director. His name was Bob Newman. The Patches show, now in its third year was in full swing, and occasionally young Newman would wander around near the set, just to watch the action. Thanks to this idle curiosity his career would soon change, drastically.

The advent of Gertrude

Hanging out near the set, Bob noticed a frequent bit used by the Clown was to grab the big phone and chat up the never seen, never heard city dump operator, Gertrude. One day when J.P. picked up the phone to see if Gertrude could send him down some food for a picnic, he dropped it. In that split second, the *J.P. Patches Show* changed forever. After J.P. picked the phone off the floor and placed his order, Bob, without warning anyone, yelled out in what would become Gertrude's trade-mark falsetto, "Okay, Julius, I'll send it right down." J.P., as surprised as anyone to hear a response, played along. Gertrude suddenly had a voice.

Back in those days, anybody who got on the show was paid $7.50 for each appearance, so everyone was looking for a chance to play a bit. Bob was no different. Hey, $7.50 was $7.50. In the early Sixties the average Joe made around $5,000 a year, and Bob saw this as an opportunity to make a few bucks on the side. He offered to pitch in doing voices, characters; anything they might need a hand with. But the catch was if you broke away from your everyday job to do something on the show you had to pay someone to cover your shift. Whether it was the lure of the limelight or that the $7.50 still made it profitable, the demand to play a bit on the show remained high.

Now that Gertrude was getting voice-time on the show, someone figured she should also have a face. Cy Flory's wife took it upon herself to whip up a

Raggedy Anne dress and a mop of red hair and handed them over to Bob. Gertrude now had the beginnings of a look. However, Bob decided that look needed a little tweaking. When Gertrude finally made her visual debut, no one had any idea what form Bob's tweaking might take. They were in for a surprise. When the moment came, Bob burst onto the set in the Raggedy Anne dress…filled with two huge balloons! While J.P. and Gertrude carried on, gravity took its toll and the balloons started drifting south. With his two big mitts, Bob grabbed the sinking balloons, quickly lifted them into place and said, "Up there big fellas."

Oops.

In 1960, breast gags on kid's shows were generally frowned upon so Chris and the crew figured that was the end of the J.P. Patches era. Parents throughout the Pacific Northwest must have simultaneously turned on their garbage disposals at that exact moment, and couldn't hear what was said, because, surprisingly, not a single complaint came in. But just to be safe, for Gertrude's next appearance, she was deflated.

The bottom line speaks

It took a couple of years but someone finally derailed the $7.50 gravy train. TV stations, like most profit driven enterprises, are notoriously tight fisted. One of the station bean-counters noticed that the directors, floor directors, and whomever else on the crew was getting paid to play a bit part on the show, was getting paid twice; once for their normal job, once for their bit part. Blasphemy. A decree came down from the upper reaches of KIRO management that Chris could hire one person to be on the show with him.

At first Chris considered Bill Gerald, who played Professor Wiener Von Brrrrown, but saw something in Bob Newman that he felt might be a better fit for the show. Bob, like the vaudeville comedians that he loved, would do anything for a laugh. Not a bad quality for a kid's show. Plus, you never knew what he would do (as Gertrude's breast-balloon-bit indicated). The man was completely unpredictable! Cy Flory remembers on more than one occasion when Bob would be going somewhere with a bit, and the early signs were pointing towards…who knows where? "The guys in the control room would begin looking at each other; nervous twitches would start breaking out. I'd tell

Craig Shreeve as Grandpa Patches, with J.P.

PATCHES MEMORIES

Jim Owens—Husky football coach (1957-74)

"On some Fridays, during football season, J.P. would use his big phone to allegedly call 'The Coach' and offer plays for his team to use for their next game. He wasn't really talking to anybody he just faked it. Well someone who had a connection with the phone company rigged it so that we could run a phone line out to the practice field we were on and I called J.P. while he was on the air. Imagine his surprise when his phone rang and he picked it up and 'The Coach' really was on the other end thanking him for all of his suggested plays in the past."

Mr. Music

Man's birthday

was celebrated

on March 4th,

and J.P.'s

birthday

was, like

all clowns,

April 1st.

Friends forever.

the audio guy to be ready to kill Bob's audio." But just when they thought Bob would say something that would leave them all looking for jobs in the morning, he would take the bit in a more kid-friendly direction, seemingly oblivious to everyone's borderline cardiacs.

He forgot to remember

To add to his unpredictability, Bob was also notorious for forgetting bits. He and Chris would be going along and suddenly he'd just blank out on where they were going with it. They didn't have a fashionable name for it in those days but Bob suffered from ADD (Attention Deficit Disorder). When Chris could see that Bob had lost his way, he would sometimes say, "Wait a minute, Gertrude, I can tell you've forgotten your lines. Let's look at the script." Of course, there never was a script for the show, so Chris would pick up the nearest piece of paper and pretend to read off it. "Let's see, the script says J.P. starts the show…and breaks up everybody. Ha, ha, ha. Ahem. J.P. is very funny, everyone loves J.P. …oh here it is, Gertrude walks in…" and Chris would then tell Bob what he was supposed to do.

Cracking up Newman

The crew loved getting a reaction out of J.P. and Gertrude. But while getting Chris to laugh was sometimes a challenge, getting Bob Newman to break up was a piece of cake. And once he started, chances are he was going down in a heap. For some reason the man simply could not laugh and keep upright. The camera operators knew if Newman started busting up they should get ready to tilt down, because he was going to be on the floor before long. In one of the most classic moments of local television, Bob Newman, as Ketchikan the Animal Man, lost it on the air while reading a children's book. You can find this bit of hilarity on a couple of the J.P. Patches videos.

It all came about when Bob, filling in for a vacationing Chris, started reading *Henny Penny*. For the first page or two, everything was going fine until

Ketchikan can't keep from cracking up.

he reached the part about Cocky-Locky (chuckle) and then Goosy-Poosy (snort), and Ducky-Daddles (guffaw). By the time he'd had to say Cocky-Locky three of four times it was all over. Sure enough, the book goes in the air and Newman goes to the ground. He desperately tried to compose himself and begin reading again, but one more line about Cocky-Locky and he was back on the floor again, holding his sides and gasping for breath. You gotta love live TV.

The history of Bob

Where Chris is a Northwest transplant, Bob is a dyed-in-the-wool, local boy. He grew up on Mercer Island, back when there were 200+ people on the island, just as many sheep, and one ferryboat. By the time he was playing football for Garfield High School, the I-90 Bridge was built so he'd either catch rides into town with his dad or he'd hitchhike in. After high school he attended the UW in 1949, but according to Bob, he was a rotten student. In 1953, during the Korean 'conflict', Bob bailed out of school and enlisted in the Marine Corps (Semper Fi, do or die). Apparently he was such a threat to North Korea they called the war off in July, forcing Bob to spend the next two years in the South Pacific and Japan, playing out his hitch in the corps. When he returned home, he finished up at the UW, then made the rounds to the different TV stations in Seattle. "Hi, I'm Bob Newman, boy do you need me!"

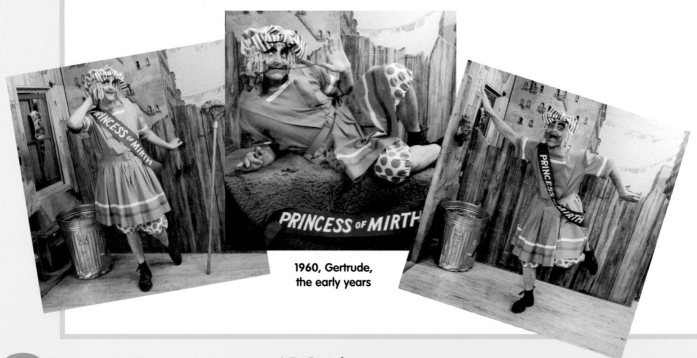

1960, Gertrude,
the early years

(slam) "Hi, I'm Bob Newman, boy do you need me!" (slam) You get the idea. Finally, KIRO-TV decided to take a chance on the brash, young marine. The station was never the same.

J.P. & Ketchikan

Over the years, Bob was known as the guy on the Patches show who played 'everyone else': the man of seventeen faces and sixteen voices (see list of characters). But his most beloved characters were the lovelorn Gertrude and Ketchikan the Animal Man, even though Bob was not the show's original animal man. That distinction goes to Jack "Uncle Jack" Armstrong, who was also one of the show's first directors. When Jack eventually left they realized that they couldn't have a kid's show without an animal guy so Bob stepped in. At first they tossed around names like Africa Jack and Congo Ken, but Bob wanted something a little more local; thus, Ketchikan Cal. Yes, you read that right, Ketchikan *Cal*. But the alliteration of 'kan' and 'man' sounded so good that Ketch's full name was seldom used.

Snakes alive!

Not to burst any bubbles, but Bob Newman didn't know a heck of a lot about animals. But according to Bob, neither did the Clown. A point, however, the Clown disputes. Regardless, between the two of them they usually had their hands full whenever something came on the set with fins, feathers or fur. And sometimes scales.

PATCHES MEMORIES

Slick Watts—Sonic Guard (1973-78)

"I did a lot of public appearances back in those days and sometimes J.P. would also be at them. If he was, it always made my job easier. He'd entertain the kids so all I had to do was sign autographs. He took all the pressure off me. In most big cities the famous people are the sports stars, but in Seattle, J.P. was the man."

Not all Patches Pals have two feet.

For one show a boa constrictor and an anaconda were to be the animals *du jour* for Ketchikan to amaze the viewers. What viewers at home didn't see, however, was that prior to the show one of the snakes took a bite out of his handler. It wasn't a poisonous snake but with a mouth the size of a catcher's mitt it could still leave a painful impression. "I guess the snakes are a little upset," noted the handler. This, of course, didn't make Chris feel any better about having them on his show, but he figured it was Newman who would be the one in danger, not him, so what the heck? When Ketchikan came on the set with one of the giant snakes draped over his shoulders, the business end of the snake was facing towards J.P. The snake, seeing the Clown's big red nose, decided it was worth investigating. So J.P. kept backing up, while Ketchikan, seemingly oblivious to the Clown's backpedaling, kept edging closer and closer until J.P. was pinned up against the wall. J.P. quickly realized that this was a perfect time for a cartoon! During the break Chris told Bob, "That's it! No more snakes!" And for the next fifteen years that edict held, that is, until they finally got a call from the Woodland Park Zoo. What happened next, according to Chris was worth the wait.

The zoo was housing the biggest snake on the West Coast and thought it would be good promotion to show it off on the Patches show. Chris agreed but told Bob, "This time I'm on the other end of the snake." So they bring on the snake, which is enormous: it must have weighed close to seventy-five pounds! J.P. was facing the camera, talking about this wonderful animal, when he began hearing strange, strangling noises from his left. A quick glance revealed that the snake had somehow managed to coil itself around Ketchikan's neck, and the animal man was turning a lovely shade of blue. After Ketch collapsed to his knees the zoo handlers raced in and finally persuaded the snake to stop killing him. It wasn't long before the phone calls started coming in about how they should be ashamed of themselves for mistreating the snake.

Boris S. Wart's pet dragon, Carmen, was named after the TV & movie composer, Carmen Dragon, who was the father of Daryl Dragon (The Captain of Captain and Tenille fame).

The problem with animals

The saying goes in the TV and movie business, "Never work with kids or animals." All J.P. Patches did was fly in the face of that conventional wisdom every single day for twenty-three years. Of course, they discovered, as the snake incident showed, there's something to be said for conventional wisdom. The only things on the show more unpredictable than Bob Newman were the kids and animals. And as anyone who's ever worked in the television industry will tell you, unpredictability makes good TV. Not always appropriate TV, but good TV. Like the time Ketchikan brought on a couple of rabbits and they started doing the wild thing on camera. Or the time a monkey became aroused. Trust me, if you saw this particular Patches show you'd remember it. Why the monkey got aroused in the first place is anyone's guess, but the humor factor took a sharp spike after Bob, who was feeding ice cream to the chimp, spilled some on the animal's, uh, unit. Needless to say, the chimp went ape. A wild, screaming frenzy quickly ensued. The chimp didn't keep quiet either. Can't say I blame him.

The poop on animal poop

The biggest problem with having animals on the show was that you never knew when they would have to poop. Actually, that's not true, according to anyone who worked on the show you always knew when an animal had to poop: the minute it walked on the set. Time after time the crew would clean up after some animal cleared out its bowels in the studio. The general rule of thumb was to not feed or water an animal before the show. Not that it made much difference. When the world famous Royal Lipizzan Stallions were

PATCHES MEMORIES

Kathi Goertzen—KOMO anchor (1980-present)
"One of my first memories of the Patches show was my fear of Gertrude. When my Bluebird troop went to the show to watch and greet J.P. and Gertrude, I remember loving J.P. and really wanting to be a good little Patches Pal, but I was always a little fearful of clowns and Gertrude seemed to intensify that fear. I think it was because he really didn't look like a she, and as a little kid, that was confusing."

making a stop in Seattle, and one of the regal beasts was slated to appear on the Patches show, Chris did his best to avert any horse-pucky problems. Before they went on the air Chris spoke with the animal's handler to make sure the horse had an opportunity to relieve itself before showtime. The handler, a little German guy named Hans, was indignant. (Please add thick German accent for best comedic results.) "Listen, Clown, dis iz a Rrroyal Lipizzan Stallion! It vill sh** vhen I tell it to sh**!" Sure enough, the minute the horse comes on the set and does a couple of tricks, it dumps its load. J.P. just looked at the horse's handler, "You were saying, Hans?"

On a similar note, as a promotion for Checkerboard Squares Boneless Turkey, a young woman came on the show with a gigantic turkey. "How big is that turkey?" asked J.P. "Forty pounds," replied the Checkerboard Squares representative. "Forty pounds?" J.P. asked. "Forty pounds," confirmed the girl. At that moment the turkey relieved itself all over the carpet. J.P. looked at the carpet, then looked at the girl, "More or less."

If it's not the animals it's the kids

There are countless middle-aged adults roaming the Pacific Northwest who know, deep down, that when they were little kids, they peed their pants on the *J.P. Patches Show*. Little girls, especially. Chris would always tell the mothers before the kids came onto the set to make sure the children first went to the bathroom. Apparently some didn't listen. When there was a Brownie Troop on the show, J.P. did his standard walk down the line of girls, tugging pigtails to the sound effect of jingling bells and asking their names. When he got to one

When cardigans & calico were all the rage:
the winners of a Red Ball Jets contest.

PATCHES TRIVIA

J.P.'s slight lisp

wasn't a conscious

effort by Chris.

The rubber nose

hampers the

movement of his

upper lip. Chris

says that without

the make-up on

he can't even

sound like J.P.

little girl in the middle she said her name, and right on cue, peed. At a commercial break, when he found the little girl crying her eyes out, Chris assured her that no one watching the show at home would ever know. "All they saw was your face," he told her. "You were so brave that I'm going to give you an extra goodie-bag." As the kids were leaving, the little girl's mother came up to Chris and told him that her daughter was embarrassed, but she really appreciated how nice he was to her, and how he cheered her up. The mother also told him that her daughter wanted to know if she could come back and pee again and get another present. Ironically, many years later, Chris was on a local radio station retelling that story when a woman called in. She was proud to say she *was* that little girl.

Since we're on the subject of bodily functions...

Peeing wasn't the only occupational hazard of working with children. Near the end of one show J.P. noticed that out of several kids who were with him on the set, one was dressed to the nines. J.P. complimented the boy on his sartorial splendor and said that his mother obviously got him dressed up for his first, big television appearance. "Oh yes!" he replied. J.P. then said, "You look so nice, but did she tell you how to act and what to do?" "Oh yes," said the boy, "be polite." J.P. then asked the boy if his mother told him what *not* to do. With perfect timing, the kid said, "Yea. Fart."

A Patches Pal gets the last laugh.

The Swami of Pastrami looks deep within his bowling, er, crystal ball.

Leroy Frump, General Handyman.

What You Didn't See

• • • • • • • • • • • • • •

Producing a daily one-hour television program is no small task. Now try doing it without a script or a budget. But that's exactly what they did with the Patches show for over two decades. The show was neither polished, nor sophisticated. Instead, it was sixty minutes of fly-by-the-seat-of-your-pants goofiness. And the elaborate preparation for that hour of goofiness began a mere half-hour before show time. Every day, about thirty minutes before they went on the air, Chris, Bob, the show's director, floor director, and audio guy would get together in the KIRO cafeteria and try to figure out what they were going to do for the show. It usually went something like this...

Chris: "So, what are we gonna do today?"

Bob: "I dunno. I came up with an idea yesterday, it's your turn."

Director: "Hey, how about the Clown can't find Esmerelda."

Chris: "Yea! And he has to bring in the Swami of Pastrami to use his psychic abilities to find her."

Bob: "But before the Clown calls the Swami he has Leroy Frump make some sort of tracking gizmo to home in on Esmerelda."

Chris: "Great! Okay, (turning to the floor director) see if you can whip up something that looks like a tracking gizmo."

Floor Director: "Uh, sure."

Sure enough, fifteen minutes later, Leroy Frump comes on the show, climbing up through the manhole, dragging his handy-dandy, high-tech 'Find-o-meter', which looks suspiciously like a cardboard box with a couple of wires sticking out of it and a few dials hastily drawn on with a felt pen.

That was usually the extent of each show's development. Whip up an idea half an hour before show time, hash out which characters will be on...and wing it. Two hours a day, five days a week, plus a show on Saturday, they winged it. Over the twenty-three year life of the show, that comes to somewhere in the neighborhood of 12,000 hours of making up stuff as they went along.

Ask anyone who worked on the show and they'll probably tell you it was the best job they ever had. "Chris valued everyone's opinion," recalls early KIRO booth announcer, Don Einarson, who also played the role of Sheriff Shot Badly in the first years of the Patches show. "He would bounce ideas off of everyone on the set. Floor director, cameraman, didn't matter. Everyone felt like they had some input, and for that reason alone I think everyone did the best work of their lives working on that show. We all had a sense of pride."

That sense of pride mixed with the pure joy of playing for a living led to a lot of laughs on the set. In fact, the laughs generated *on* camera were frequently generated because of what happened *off* camera. A good-humored battle between Chris and the crew was waged on a daily basis. Chris loved to mess with the crew and the crew loved to mess with the Clown. There was only one rule: don't detract from the show. Everyone working on the *J.P. Patches Show* had a blast, but it was understood that the fun would never be at the expense of the viewer. What you *didn't* see on the screen was frequently funnier than what you did see. For example…

It almost sounds like…

Bill Gerald (Professor Wiener Von Brrrrown) was the man most responsible for cracking up the Clown. He just seemed to know how to push Chris's funny-button. During one broadcast he took a bucket of water and snuck

The many moods of the mayor.

around beside the set where he couldn't be seen. The Clown could hear him but didn't have any idea what he was up to. Bill then slowly trickled the water from one bucket into another. The microphone couldn't pick it up, but to J.P., trying desperately to stifle a laugh, it sounded like someone taking a whiz just outside the door.

If at first you don't succeed...

Speaking of water, it seemed to play a role in an awful lot of the pranks pulled on the Clown. To many crewmembers, any day J.P. got wet was a good day. There were many good days. But after getting soaked time and time again the Clown grew wise to the crew's booby-traps and watery schemes, even when they disguised their efforts under the camouflage of daily routine.

The floor director knew the afternoon show always started the same way: J.P. roles up to the magic house on his tricycle and crashes into the garbage can. Every day, like clockwork. Clown rides in, hits can, falls off trike, camera shakes. So one day the floor director pushes J.P. on the trike and right before he hits the can the Clown slams on the brakes. He could see that the crew had filled the garbage can with water. J.P. turns to the camera, looking as smug as a person can look with a big red, rubber nose and says, "Looks like the magic house is trying to play a trick on ol' J.P." Score: J.P.-1, Crew-0. The crew, however, like a band of bad-seed Boy Scouts, were prepared. They had a plan-B. Seconds later one of the set walls, strategically loosened, came crashing down on J.P., nearly knocked him cold. Smug look gone; score tied.

Sturdley awaits a light lunch of literature

Sturdley, before cosmetic surgery.

...but will settle for a clown-crunchy.

The forecast calls for rain

As the falling set piece that knocked J.P. silly showed, gravity was a great way to deliver a gag's sucker punch. Above the set was a crisscrossing network of pipes from which the lights were hung. Frequently, the crew found other things to hang up there as well. Like water balloons. They'd hang them over every square inch of the set, so no matter where the Clown was standing he was always in the bullseye. And the Clown knew they were up there. On the days the balloons were hanging he knew he was at their mercy. The crew's weapon of choice for popping the water balloons was either a long, needle

PATCHES MEMORIES

Gary Locke——Governor of Washington State (1997-present)

"My friends and I would watch Patches when we were in college. The show always had a lot of adult humor and double entendres and we'd be thinking, *'How can they get away with some of this stuff on a kid's show?'*"

tipped stick, or blow-darts, which they would leave out in full view, just to remind the Clown that anytime could be shower time. Before long the Clown's most used prop on the set was an umbrella.

Newman says, "Cheese"

The Clown wasn't the only cast member with 'kick me' taped to his back. Bob Newman was just as inviting. And frequently the perpetrator of the gag was Bill Gerald.

One of his more 'tasteful' jokes centered on a live commercial they did for Keds Sneakers. For the commercial they would role the famous military film clip from the Sixties of the guy wearing a jetpack, taking to the air. In a full, face-covering helmet and jetpack, the man would lift off and fly away. At this point they'd cut back to J.P. on set saying, "That sounds like Commander Keds!" The next thing you know, Bob walks in the door wearing the same outfit: Commander Keds. The bit always ran pretty smoothly, but on the day the commercial was running for its last time, Bob couldn't find the helmet. Seconds before Bob was supposed to go on, Bill Gerald miraculously finds the helmet and tosses it to Bob. By the time Bob was on camera he made the pungent realization that Bill had smeared Limburger cheese inside the helmet. J.P., of course, could smell it from where he was (heck, the guys in the control room could probably smell it), so

Boris S. Wart, second meanest man in the world.

while Bob desperately looked for an excuse to get out of the helmet ("Look at the time! Commander Keds had better be going.") the Clown was saying, "Gee, Commander Keds, since this is your last day you really should stick

That's funny. He was in this coffin a few minutes ago.

around for awhile." For the rest of the day, Bob stank like the front window of a Long Island deli on the hottest day of the year.

If I had a hammer...

For pranks and practical jokes the crew had a distinct advantage over the Clown in that he was only at the station a few hours a day. That left plenty of time for any crewmember to implement whatever devious ploy he had up his sleeve. And all props were open game. Of course, being that the set was one big landfill of props, for J.P. it was like walking through a practical joke mine-field. Who knew what might be wired, rigged or...nailed?

On one show J.P.'s big phone started ringing, but when he tried to pick it up it wouldn't budge. Before he had a chance to even scratch his head in puzzlement there was a knock at the door. When he tried to open it, that too wouldn't budge. Suddenly, Esmerelda's crying. He goes to pick her up off the table but she's stuck! Wait, now Griswald's barking. By this time the Clown knew it wouldn't do any good to try to pick up Griswald either. Just like everything else on the set, he knew Griswald would be nailed down.

Our little girl is growing up

Esmerelda was always a popular target for the crew's antics. They would hide her in any number of places around the set. They also knew the audio guy could help trigger the search. Mr. Music Man (Duane Smart) frequently led the Clown by playing a specific sound effect. If he played the phone ringing, the Clown would answer the phone. If he played Esmerelda's laugh, the Clown would usually make a quick look around for her. But on one show the crew used Tikey Turkey as bait for an Esmerelda gag. When Mr. Music Man played Tikey's gobble, J.P. took that as his cue to go check on the rubber turkey. But when he opened the oven door to get Tikey he found Esmerelda inside instead…wearing a bra!

The new cameraman

Practical jokes and wise cracks were *de rigueur* on the set, but no one was ever heckled or embarrassed to the point of being offended. Not that the opportunities didn't arise.

For a bit with the Clown and resident handy-

The secret words to open Ggoorrsstt's secret room were 'Zabba, zabba, zabba, zoo, secret room, alla-ka-zoo'. Bob Newman named his boat the Zabba, Zabba.

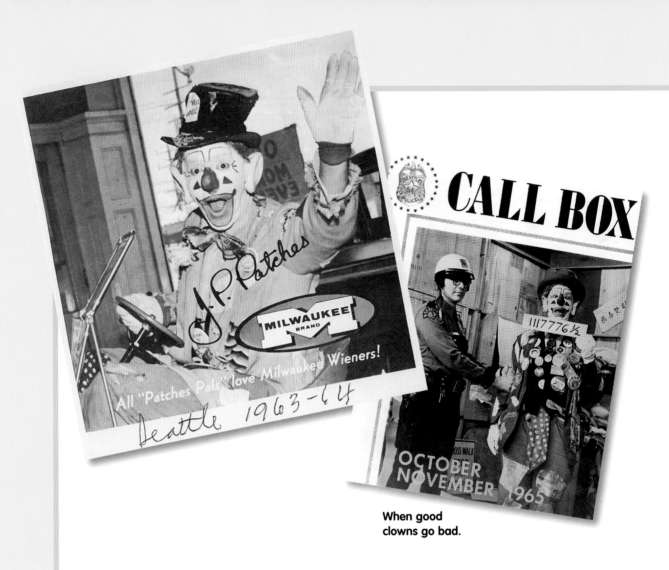

**When good
clowns go bad.**

man Leroy Frump, a new cameraman was on the job. When it was time for
Leroy to make his appearance, J.P. unfolded the black piece of paper that acted
as Leroy's manhole, and laid it on the floor for Leroy Frump to send his ladder up through. I hate to shatter the illusion for you but the molecular make-
up of paper does not lend itself to act as a form of portal, letting matter pass
through it without some form of resistance. Someone must have forgotten to
tell the new cameraman. For Leroy Frump's paper manhole bit the standard
practice was for the cameraman to keep the shot on J.P. after he laid down the
paper. This way Bob Newman could shove a ladder up in front of the camera

PATCHES MEMORIES

Dan Evans—Governor of Washington State (1965-77)

"I remember talking to J.P. and telling him, 'You're the luckiest guy
in the world. You are probably as recognized as I am, if not more,
but when you take off the costume and make-up you can walk
the street and nobody knows who you are. And to top it off, they
don't heckle you about tax increases.'"

to make it look like it just popped up out of the hole, then Leroy would climb up. But when J.P laid the paper hole on the floor, the new cameraman instinctively tilted the camera down to the hole…and stayed there, apparently waiting for the ladder to miraculously pop up through the paper. I sort of wonder how long he would have held that shot if J.P. didn't tell him, on the air, that Leroy didn't really come up through the paper hole.

The Clown's revenge

The crew may have had their tactical advantages for messing with the Clown but J.P. had his own methods of revenge. Since J.P. ran the show most everything and everybody reacted to him. Sometimes he took advantage of that.

When Bob Newman was on the show playing Ketchikan, J.P. might say, "I better call Gertrude." He'd walk over to the phone and Newman, now off camera, would have to change over to Gertrude's voice. Then J.P. would walk back over to Newman and say, "I've got Gertrude on the phone." Newman would say, "Yea, that's great", in Ketchikan's voice. Then the Clown would walk over a little to get Newman off camera so Newman could go back to being Gertrude, so then J.P. would ask Gertrude if he could speak with Boris

J.P. with the mother of modeling agents, Lola Hallowell.

When the secret room opened, the 'Ooga-chugga singers' would start singing (Blue Swede's Hooked on a Feeling). J.P. referred to the 'singers' as Patti, Maxine, and Laverne: the Andrew Sisters.

S. Wart, forcing Newman to change to another voice. Of course, J.P. would continue doing this as many times as he could get away with it.

Everyone was fair game, even the audio guy, sitting fifty feet away behind glass in a booth. J.P. might say, "I think I hear Miss Smith coming," forcing the audio guy to find the sound effect for Miss Smith's motorcycle. Then the Clown would say, "No wait, I think I also hear Chief MoonRay," sending the audio guy scrambling for another sound effect. In the first few seasons the audio guy

J.P. & his right-hand, er, woman.

Ggoorrsstt, Griswald & J.P.

didn't have the benefit of sound effects dubbed off onto tapes, he actually had records and would have to find the right record and drop the needle in the right groove, all in a matter of seconds. This led to a great deal of gnashing of teeth and shaking of fists.

As the episode with the cameraman and Leroy Frump's manhole indicated, new crewmembers were a favorite target. When Duane Smart took over the job as Mr. Music Man, J.P. left the poor guy with a case of the flop sweats.

Young, inexperienced, still wet behind the ears, Duane was very excited about his big chance to run audio for the show. But on Duane's first day, when the Clown walked onto the set and began talking…no sound came out. His mouth was moving but you couldn't hear a word! Poor Duane, his first day on the job and within seconds he thinks he's single-handedly humiliated Seattle's most popular television personality. His heart rate was redlining like a '72 Buick on a cop-free stretch of I-90 blacktop. Duane's panic attack finally came to an end when, seconds later, J.P.'s voice cut through the deadly silence. As it turns out, the microphones worked fine. It was just the Clown screwing with him.

His favorite target

Since the show wasn't scripted, the camera operators and floor directors were never precisely sure what J.P. and Gertrude were going to do, but after awhile they got a feel for where things were headed. Plus, J.P. was good about projecting what he was going to do. This helped the camera operators keep two steps ahead of the Clown and one step ahead of the director.

Of course, J.P. never wanted them to get too comfortable. It was the floor director, the person down by the set, who usually ended up at the business end of one of the Clown's gags. The floor director was in charge of getting props, moving the boom-microphone around the set, and cueing the Clown: in other words, a convenient, within-arms-reach, whipping boy.

J.P.'s favorite torment was to constantly move back and forth across the set, forcing the floor director to chase after him with the boom-microphone. Then, to make things even dicier, J.P. would do something that demanded the

PATCHES MEMORIES

Greg Nickels—Mayor of Seattle (2001-present)
"In 1961, when I was six years old, my family moved here from Erie, Pennsylvania (the best thing that ever happened to our family) and we were staying at the Chief Seattle motel on East Marginal Way until our house was ready to occupy. My younger brothers, Mark and Pete, and I turned on the TV that first morning and there was J.P. as big as life in glorious black and white. It was great! Unlike anything we had experienced in Erie! As the Mayor of the city dump he could well have been the role model for my early involvement in politics."

No, I asked the make up guy for a little mousse!

floor director's participation. Out of the blue, he might say he felt like checking on Ggoorrsstt, forcing the floor director to set the mike, run around behind the set, kick open the secret room door, shake the walls and run back around to move the mike again. Of course, by this time the Clown had moved back to the far side of the set, calling out for Guardian Elephant, which meant the floor director had to race back, find the duct-tube that acted as Guardian's trunk and stick that through the Dutch door.

If nothing else, working on the set of the *J.P. Patches Show* got you in great shape. If the Clown did too many trips back and forth, that was when the floor director would go grab a bucket and walk over to the studio water spigot and fill it. Hearing the water running into the bucket usually sent a message to the Clown. But according to long time floor director and sometime show director, Rick Jones, "Just having the bucket on the floor next to me was warning enough."

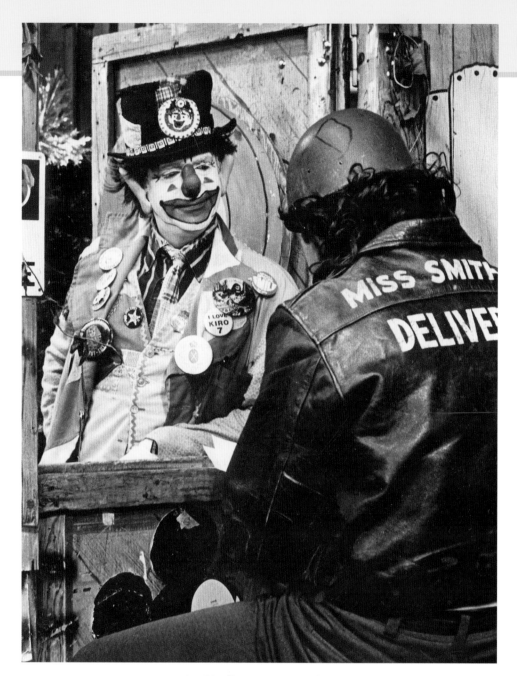

Is it a hit (ding) or a miss? (clunk)

Ding? Or Clunk?

Whenever the Clown and Miss Smith were playing *Is it a hit* (ding) *or a miss?* (clunk), J.P. would use the opportunity to see how well the floor director was paying attention. The Clown would be talking with Miss Smith, describing the game and trying to get the floor director, who was sitting a few feet away, off camera, holding the hammer, the bell and the bucket that made the sound effects, to make the wrong sound. He'd say, "You know, Miss Smith, when you play *Is it a hit* (ding) *or a miss?* (clunk), you need to get a

(ding) twice to win, but if you get a (clunk) twice you lose. So it's imperative that you get a (ding) instead of a (clunk) otherwise you'll lose, and we all know what can happen when you get a (clunk) twice, instead of a (ding) twice." This would go on and on for several minutes, and made some of the funniest moments in Patches' history. Check out the Patches Memories videotape for a stellar example.

Cracking up the Clown

J.P. Patches made a living out of making people laugh, so the crew thought it only fitting that they should try to get a chuckle out of the laughmaker, himself. They lived for the moment. It didn't happen often but they knew they had him going when they could actually see his teeth. That was the litmus test, seeing teeth.

Duane Smart, (Mr. Music Man) recalls how he finally got to the Clown with a bit involving Esmerelda. "When Esmerelda laughed you heard the standard *tee-hee*. Esmerelda's little brother

Joe Towey directing the Patches show.

When the Swami of Pastrami ran out of Twinkle Dust, J.P. invited kids to send some in. Kids from all over the area began sending in their own version of Twinkle Dust. A few days later Chris was visited at the station by postal employees telling him to stop having kids send in Twinkle Dust. The kids were sending in envelopes full of dirt, sand, confetti and whatever else they figured looked like Twinkle Dust, and it was ruining the post office canceling machines.

Before "the frito-bandito", there was "the corn-chip-clown".

and sister, Irving and Isolde, laughed the same way as Esmerelda, but since they were smaller I played it at 45 instead of 33rpms. But on one show J.P. heard a knock at the door and when he opened it there was a giant Esmerelda doll, nearly six feet tall! This was a surprise to everyone in the booth — I think the Clown, too. But I quickly grabbed the Esmerelda sound effect record, cued it up, and spun it reeeeeal slow, by hand. The sound that came out sounded like Esmerelda on Quaaludes. The director, Joe Towey, nearly fell out of his chair. The technical director was in tears on the switcher and as for J.P.? Lots of teeth."

The almost naked woman

This next story has been passed around and embellished for so many years it has become a bit of an urban legend. What really happened, sad to say, is not nearly as racy as what people think. It all started, like many Patches stories, with a knock at the magic house door. J.P. wasn't expecting anyone, but that was hardly new with the way they played it fast and loose. When he opened it he was genuinely surprised to see an attractive young woman who worked at the station, standing there in a long coat. Bear in mind, viewers at home couldn't see who was outside the door. Not knowing what she was doing there, but figuring he could get some mileage out of it, J.P. invited her in. She refused. Puzzled, he asked why. That's when she opened her coat to reveal that she was wearing nothing but a bra and a pair of men's boxers. And to top it off her body was covered with writing (Think Goldie Hawn on *Laugh-In.* Arrows pointing to belly button: 'push here', etc.).

The Clown didn't bat an eye. He played it off as if a neighbor had just come by to visit the city dump but didn't have time to come in for a visit. He said goodbye and went on with the show, while the crew beat their heads against the walls for not being able to shake him up on camera.

The completely naked woman

There was one other occasion where a scantily clad woman impacted the show, but this time she was more scantily and less clad. Hal Willard, the man behind the smooth-as-silk baritone voice of Mr. Announcer Man (or as some people called him, Mr. 'Nouncer Man) was celebrating his birthday, and for the occasion someone in his family arranged for a stripper to show up in his booth. Sure enough, at the precise moment that J.P. donned the Radar Ears and greeted Mr. Announcer Man with the standard gong and bow, a beautiful woman waltzed into the audio booth wearing nothing but a smile.

Part of Mr. Announcer Man's schtick with J.P., after he gave the weather forecast, was to try to stump him with a bit of *'by the way'* trivia. On this day, everyone on the staff half expected Mr. Announcer Man's trivia to run along the lines of, "By the way, J.P., what do the numbers 36-24-36 stand for?" Instead, like a true professional, Hal avoided the temptation, gamely weathered the distraction, and no one at home was the wiser. The only giveaway, perhaps, may have been a more pronounced smile in Mr. Announcer Man's voice.

Live vs. taped

Without scripts the Patches show tended to be about as unpredictable as a Gaylord Perry spitball. But that's the beauty of live television. Mistakes were right out there for everyone to see, and as they say in the biz, the camera never blinks.

PATCHES MEMORIES

Stan Boreson—Host of KING's Klubhouse, (1954-67)

"I remember surprising Chris on his birthday by bursting in on his show with my accordion, singing *Happy Birthday*. Things were a lot looser in those days. Can you imagine someone from KING-TV appearing on a KIRO-TV show nowadays? I didn't even ask KING management for permission, I just showed up because Chris was my friend."

Ggoorrsstt's costume was originally made with three arms, one on each side and one in front in the middle. This way Bob Newman could be constantly changing which arms he's putting his arms into. The only problem was that if he wasn't using the middle arm it hung down in front like a giant uh, well, just imagine. The third arm was quickly removed. By the way, if you've ever wondered just what that was on Ggoorrsstt's face, it was a big eyeball with an eyebrow above it. Yea, I was never quite sure either. His feet were swim fins with the tips chopped off.

The show, however, wasn't always live. Video tape recorders were invented in 1956, but most stations didn't use them on a regular basis until several years later, when the quality was suitable for something more than showing off the industry's new high tech gimmick.

It wasn't until 1960 that KIRO could afford the luxury of taping a Patches show on occasion. Once they got comfortable with this new technology they began taping the Saturday Patches show in advance, but still, the vast majority of the weekday Patches shows you saw at home were happening as you watched them. Even when a show was done live, they usually rolled tape on it anyway, but every week they'd just tape over the previous week's worth of shows. That's why there are only a few hours of Patches video in existence.

The live aspect made for good television, but taping the show did offer one benefit: it gave them the opportunity to do a little pre-broadcast chopping, if need be. The cast and crew had always gotten away with a lot of double entendres and *'nudge, nudge, wink-wink'* material, but every now and then they crossed the line. It didn't happen often, but occasionally something got edited out of the show.

Before one such show Bob Newman told Chris he didn't have a joke for the Miss Smith *'Is it a hit* (ding) *or a miss?* (clunk)' bit. So Chris says, "Ask me what 5Q plus 5Q equals, and I'll answer, '10Q'. Then you say 'You're velcome.'" (add laff here). So they're in the show and Miss Smith roles up to the city dump and tell the joke like they practiced. Blah, blah, blah…you're velcome. Ha,

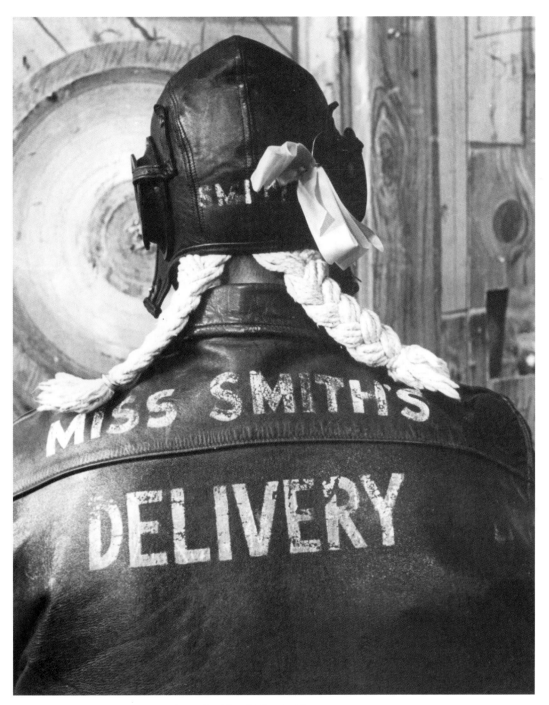

The only side of Miss Smith you ever saw.

ha, ha. But before the Clown is even finished doing his Patches chuckle, Miss Smith jumps in with another joke. "Hey, Snookie Poo, what's 2Q plus 2Q?" J.P. quickly does the math and says, "4Q." It never made it on the air.

Paying the Bills

• • • • • • • • • • • • • •

Thirty seconds of commercial time in the 2002 Super Bowl cost two million dollars. For the client, that two million didn't even include what it cost to produce the commercial. My, how times have changed.

In the early days of television, commercials were done live, by the show's host. The entire financial outlay for production costs hovered right around zero. All they did was set up a sign with the product's name on it and the pitchman did the rest. The Patches show was no different. During a cartoon, the floor director would set up a display, and J.P. would stand next to it and tout the virtues of said product. Hansen's Sunbeam Bread, Darigold Milk and Milwaukee Meats were some of the Clown's most devout sponsors.

But as we keep seeing, live television has its own unique risks.

The Hi-C incident

In today's ultra-bottom-line-oriented television climate, the idea of messing with a client's commercial is heresy. Apparently that wasn't as much of an issue in the old days. When J.P. was doing a live commercial for Hi-C Juice he enthusiastically praised the fine juice drink and took a big swig from a cup the floor director had poured for him …spiked with vodka! Chris nearly blew it across the set.

During a break J.P. confronted the floor director and suggested that he, not the floor director, open the can and pour his own juice from then on. So the next day, when it was time for another Hi-C commercial, J.P. walked over to the display, picked up the can, opened it, poured himself a glass and chugged it down…and nearly sprayed it across the set again. The night before, the floor director punched a hole in the bottom of the can, drained out some of the Hi-C, pumped in some vodka with a syringe and soldered the hole closed.

More problems with punch

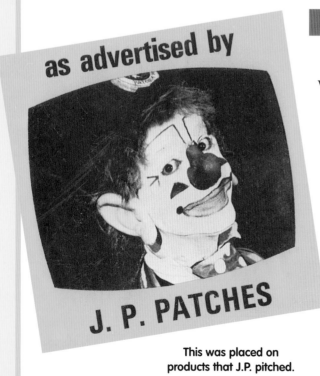

This was placed on products that J.P. pitched.

Before his days as J.P. Patches, when Chris was in Minneapolis doing his bit as Joe the Cook, Chris was promoting a juice product called *Billy Boy Punch*. One day the guy who owned the company called Chris in a panic, asking if him if he was doing a Billy Boy Punch commercial on the show that day. Chris said he was. The man told him, "Don't do it!" Chris asked why, but the man just said under no circumstances was he

to do the live commercial on his show. Chris later discovered that the grape Billy Boy Punch was fermenting on the shelves! The owner was afraid that if Chris kept pitching his product he was going to have a bunch of drunken kids on his hands. Not to mention a few lawsuits.

Plan-B for Bread

For the Patches show, improvisation was the order of the day, and sometimes that applied to commercials, too. Retired producer Alex Crewdsen recalls an incident when they were shooting a commercial for Hansen's Sunbeam Bread. "The agency wasn't good about sending over fresh bread, so I sent out another crew member to buy some at the store, but all he could find was Wonder Bread. We ended up stuffing Wonder Bread slices into an empty Sunbeam wrapper."

Milking it

Watch some of the videotapes of the Patches show and you realize they screwed up a lot. Of course, that was part of the show's charm. But sometimes what looked like a mistake was actually just a cleverly planned bit by the Clown.

On almost every show there was a Brownie troop or some group of kids that was invited to be on after the last cartoon. They would watch the show from behind soundproof glass and then come onto the set at the end of the show. On one show, right before a group of kids was brought onto the set, J.P. came up to the soundproof room to get a volunteer to help him do a live commer-

Tikey Turkey (who looked suspiciously like a rubber chicken) was originally named Kevin Turkey after audio guy Kevin Blazina, but parents with kids named Kevin kept calling in and complaining that their children were being harassed at school. Kevin Turkey was then renamed Tikey Turkey. Tikey lived in J.P.'s oven.

cial. Every kid in the room went nuts, but J.P. chose, to the puzzlement of everyone in there, the one kid who wasn't jumping up and down. When the cartoon ended J.P. brought the boy onto the set to help him with a Darigold milk commercial. J.P. pitched the product, telling all the Patches Pals at home how Darigold was good for stuff like strong bones and teeth. He poured the boy a glass and after he drank it down J.P. told him, "Show the boys and girls how good Darigold milk is for your teeth." The boy gave the camera a big smile, revealing a mouth full of missing teeth! The Clown quickly slapped a gloved hand over the kid's mouth

The end of live commercials

Julius Pierpont Patches may well have been the greatest pitchman in Seattle's history. When J.P hawked a product, kids bought it. That made for very happy clients, but for a very unhappy political action group.

It was called *Action for Children's Television*, and in the late Sixties they made it their mission to stop TV personalities from brainwashing children into becoming capitalist minions. In response to

J.P. with one of his most devout sponsors, Hansen's Bakery.

the threat of legislation, the Patches show stopped J.P. from directly selling products. Of course, they didn't say anything about J.P.'s relatives. So Grandma and Grandpa Patches quickly stepped in as commercial hucksters, but it didn't take long to see that they didn't have the same consumer cache' as J.P. Live commercials soon went the way of the twenty five cent cup of coffee and the fifteen minute commute.

PATCHES MEMORIES

John Keister—Host of Almost Live on KING (1984-99)

"My most powerful J.P. memory begins in the third grade. The den mothers in our Cub Scout pack announced that they had signed us up to be visitors on the show. We were very excited. In those days seeing J.P. at the Seafair parade or a grocery store opening was like meeting the Pope. We thought we would be going in the next day or so but then we were informed that the wait was a little over nine months. Nine Cub Scout months is equivalent to the time it takes Halley's Comet to return to earth. We quickly forgot all about it.

"At that time my father was involved in a business that sold agricultural equipment and we occasionally visited the apple growing region of Washington. During one of those visits I got to cut school. I was elated until my mother told me that this was the day our Cub Scout den was visiting the J.P. Patches Show. What? They were at J.P.'s house and I was in Wenatchee?

"I tuned in the show and wept at the sight of my buddies standing there with their goody bags shaking hands with J.P. As silly as this sounds I've never forgotten that moment. It was honestly one of the biggest disappointments of my life."

Like Sinatra, only funnier.

The Sounds of the Show

• • • • • • • • • • • • • •

What you *heard* on the show may have been just as important as any schtick you *saw* on the show. The audio set the mood, filled in the gaps, provided punch lines, and gave the characters something to respond to. If the *J.P. Patches Show* was an ice cream sundae, the music and sound effects were the whipped cream and crushed nuts. They made it complete.

In the first years of the show, a gentleman named Bob Hoagland ran audio, and the equipment was, shall we say, primitive. Just about every piece of audio was played off a record, and if Bob saw that the Clown needed a sound effect, pronto, he had to find the right record and drop the needle in the right groove at the precise moment that it was required. After Bob left the show, and eventually helped pioneer slo-motion technology with ABC, Kevin Blazina took over. (Kevin was instrumental in Tikey Turkey's beginnings, but more on that in Patches Trivia) Then, in 1966, after a couple more audio guys had brief stints with the show, Duane Smart took over the musical reins. For the next fifteen years he was the omnipresent Mr. Music Man.

Torturing Mr. Music Man

As the years went by the equipment got a little better, but that didn't mean the job was any less challenging. J.P. knew what equipment the audio man had in the booth, knew what was at his disposal, and the limitations. He frequently tested those limitations. The Clown liked to do what Duane referred to as "role call," where he would come onto the show and check to see if all the usual characters were on hand, because each character was associated with a specific sound effect. "Esmerelda? (tee-hee) Griswald? (bark, bark) Tikey Turkey? (gobble, gobble) Topokity Bird? (I'm not sure how to describe Topokity's sound effect.)" According to Joe Towey, the show's director for most of those years, it's unfortunate they never shot any video of what was going on in the audio booth during these moments: tapes and records fly-

One of Gertrude's

tin crowns

sleeps with the

fishes. Bob was

stepping off his

boat on Lake

Union, enroute

to a public

appearance

and...whoops,

whoops, whoops

...ker-plunk!

ing all over the place as Duane scrambled to get the appropriate sound effect on at the right time.

To follow along with the show, Duane had a video monitor in his booth but seldom watched it. Looking at the monitor was time he would need looking at tape labels, so instead of watching what was going on on the set, he listened. It got to the point where it was like mental telepathy between Duane and the Clown. Duane would usually know what sound effect was needed before J.P. even hinted at it.

Mr. Music Man strikes back!

If the Clown was enjoying himself a little too much, putting Duane through his paces, Duane had his own ways of letting him know to knock it off. When Mr. Music Man finally had enough, he would ring the big phone and when J.P. answered it Duane would play the short audio outtake, "Oh, I'm little Johnny Everything. I can be most anything!" When J.P. heard Little Johnny Everything he knew that it was time to stop.

Duane had a couple of other sound effects he would use when it was time to draw the line. Sometimes he'd play The Little Spinach Girl (Shirley Temple saying, "Excuse me, did I hear you say spinach?") or Buffalo Bob from the *Howdy Doody Show* ("Hey kids, what time is it?"). If Mr. Music Man reeeeally needed to shut up the Clown, he'd ring the phone and play the voice of the show's mythical director, Sam Gefeltafish, which was actually just a sped up vinyl-disc recording of an Arm and Hammer Baking Soda

J.P. with a phone, cleverly disguised as a banana.

commercial. The sped up, undecipherable words became the voice of Sam, usually chewing out J.P., telling him to move along with the show.

Something that Duane started doing that became a staple of the show that most people might not even have consciously noticed, was the show's background music. Throughout the show Mr. Music Man played soft, incidental background music just to give the different bits their own distinct flavor. Check out J.P.'s final show on videotape and you'll hear what I'm talking about: subtle, but effective.

Watch out for that hole!

For the true audiophiles who've always wanted to know, a lot of the show's sound effects came off of the High Fidelity series called, *Doctored for Super Sound*. Another favorite source was a Disney record called *Thrilling, Chilling Sounds of the Haunted House*, which supplied the sound for whenever someone fell into the giant hole outside J.P.'s front door.

Speaking of which, that sound effect caused more than its share of trouble. Whenever anyone left the magic house during a show, J.P. would always remind him to look out for the hole, and of course, a moment later you'd hear the sound of them screaming as they supposedly fell in. To any kid watching at home, it made for great laughs…unless, of course, it happened to be someone you actually knew. Just ask the kids of Officer Friendly.

Officer Friendly was a real-life cop who came on and told kids to stay away from strangers or not to play in the street. He was a show staple for many years, and every time he left the show, you'd hear him fall in the hole. On the first show employing a new Officer Friendly, a younger man who replaced the original, J.P. dutifully told him to watch out for the hole on his way out. Cue sound effect. Little did he know that at that moment, his kids were at home crying their eyes out, thinking that their dad had actually fallen into the hole.

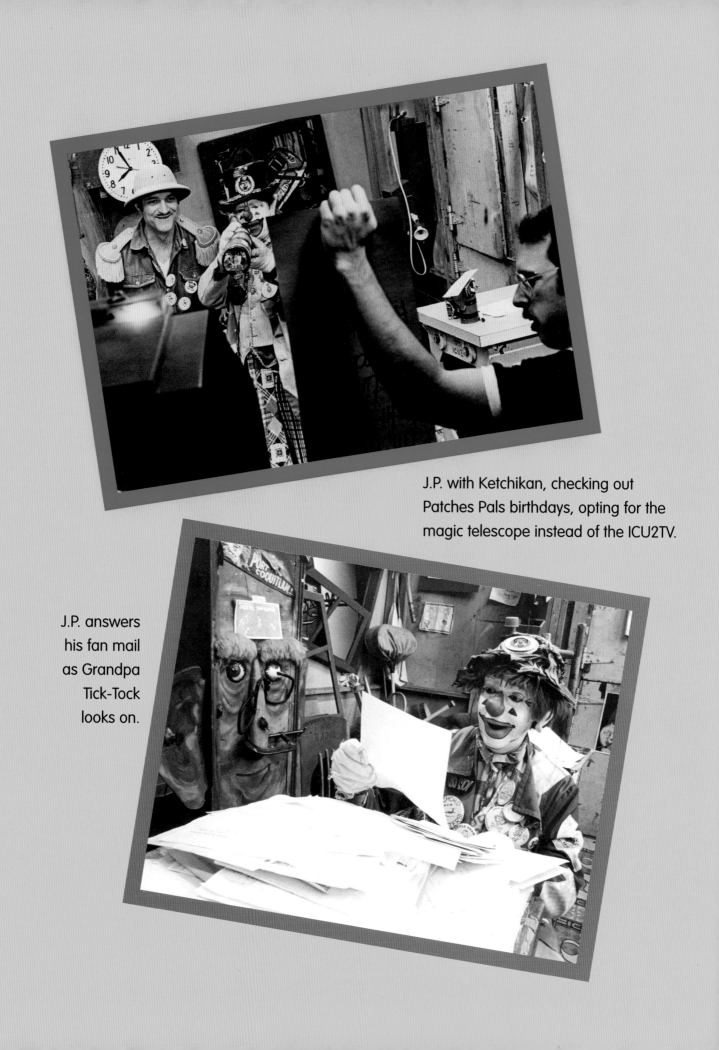

J.P. with Ketchikan, checking out Patches Pals birthdays, opting for the magic telescope instead of the ICU2TV.

J.P. answers his fan mail as Grandpa Tick-Tock looks on.

More Than Just Props

· · · · · · · · · · · · · ·

The *J.P. Patches Show*, flat out, had no budget. What they had to spend on props could hardly cover the cost of three slices of pizza and a pack of Trident. But that was part of the appeal. J.P.'s shack by the city dump was such a hodge-podge of clutter that something new and shiny would have seemed crass and out of place. Every prop used on the show was held together with duct tape and baling wire. Grandpa Tick-Tock's eyeballs were croquet balls, cut in half. For a *Star Wars* bit, R2D2 was played by a Shop-Vac. When they did an underwater bit, they held a fishtank full of water in front of the camera and hung cardboard sharks from the ceiling. That worked fine until the sharks spun around and you could see 'Safeway' printed on the back.

It was this type of velvet-Elvis charm that viewers came to love. The *J.P. Patches Show* hit on that magic intangible that eludes so many failures: it wasn't aware of its shortcomings. The Patches show was kitschy and had no idea.

Every set piece, every prop, every costume became so familiar to us, that we came to know the inside of the magic house better than we knew our own bedroom. The difference was our window couldn't spin, our clocks didn't talk, our phones weren't three feet tall, and our carpet didn't have a checkers game woven into it. It was a magic room where everything had a personality all its own.

ICU2TV set

Slap together a plywood box, cut a hole in the front, add a couple of knobs and, *voila!* a magic TV set.

The ICU2TV was probably the most well known prop on the show. J.P. would hunker down in front of it and could see whose birthday it was, and maybe even where the birthday boy or girl might find a special present hidden. (They always seemed to be in the dryer)

The ICU2TV was also a kind of low-rent transporter. J.P. could climb in and it would take him to Santa's workshop at the North Pole. From where we were sitting at home, on the gold shag carpet, in our Underoos, the ICU2TV was magical, exciting and just a little terrifying. You'd think, how could this clown look into his TV and see me? More than a few kids throughout the Northwest were known to hide behind their dad's La-Z-Boy when J.P.

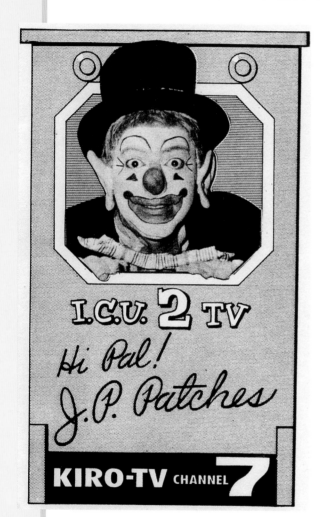

plopped down in front of his magical TV set.

Every year on your birthday you desperately wished to hear J.P. speak your name. But that only happened if your mom or dad called in, days or weeks in advance to put your name on the list. In the early years of the show, J.P. would read a kid's first *and* last name, but Chris decided it was better if they only used first names after the crew began slipping in fake names (Mike Sass, Warren Peece, Pete Moss, Jim Shorts). The crew also wasn't above holding up pictures from certain adult magazines, trying to break up the Clown.

One time the ICU2TV was even the subject of crime-tip sent in to the Tacoma Police Department. According to the police, someone called to see if they were aware of a heinous activity in which J.P. Patches was involved. "What exactly is J.P. doing?" the police asked the caller. "You know when he's using the ICU2TV set, and reading off kid's names and ages?" the caller cryptically asked the police, "Well, he's actually giving signals for a dope drop!" Needless to say, the next day when J.P. sat down in front of the ICU2TV the crew made sure the birthday list read something like, "Suzy is 8 today. Mikey is 5. Bring a dime bag to Fourth and Pine…"

The Pal-a-Vac

We only got to see it a couple of months a year, but it never failed to hold our attention every time it was brought out: the Pal-a-Vac!

Whenever Christmas season rolled around, the infamous Pal-a-Vac made its appearance. It was a large box with J.P.'s face on the front, and was used to determine if a child was naughty or nice. J.P. would drop in the child's letter to Santa, turn the crank, and if the child was good J.P.'s nose and eyes on the box would light up and his bow tie would wiggle. If the child was naughty, J.P.'s smile would flip upside down into a frown and a horrendous buzzer would sound.

The box was a classic Rube Goldberg contraption thrown together with duct tape, coffee cans and bungee chords. The buzzer was a warning bell taken off a submarine and the spinning mouth was rigged up to a gigantic magnetic solenoid. Kids would send in their letters to Santa and, of course, they were always rated 'nice'. But for the bit to be funny there had to be some kids rated as 'naughty'. At first they came up with fake names of naughty kids, but that backfired when, inevitably, some kid watching at home with the same name would run screaming to his mother, who would then call, screaming at J.P. They eventually used the names of people that everyone agreed were naughty. People like Boris, or Zenobia (gasp!) or maybe even J.P. if he was doing something bad, like trying to see his name in Santa's book. When they tossed in a letter from KIRO station manager, Lloyd Cooney, the Pal-a-Vac blew up.

When Grandpa Tick-Tock would talk, the director would cut back and forth between a close up of the clock and a wide shot of J.P. standing in front, talking to the clock. They would have to use close ups of the clock because it was actually J.P. doing the talking so he'd have to watch a monitor off camera to make sure the director had cut to a close up of the clock before he'd talk in Grandpa Tick-Tock's voice. Then to top it off, Bob Newman, who was normally moving Grandpa Tick-Tock's mouth from behind couldn't see J.P. talking so he would just have to guess when the Clown would talk and for how long. To hedge his bets he would always leave the mouth halfway open.

The Peek-a-Vue

Part of the genius of the Patches show was the Clown and company knew how to cover their bases. They always left themselves an out. They didn't make Boris S. Wart the first meanest man in the world because someone would always say there's someone meaner. If J.P. and the gang were in a fix they could always call on the Swami of Pastrami because he had magical powers and magical powers can take care of pretty much anything. See? Always an out.

Then there was the Peek-a-Vue. It looked like a built-in TV set with a blue screen, and J.P. used it to call Santa at the North Pole, or anyone else he wanted to talk to, face-to-face, if the person wasn't handy. Talk about hedging your bets. The Peek-a-Vue gave the Clown the ability to contact darn near anyone. It was brilliant! For a kid back in the Seventies it seemed like magic. Nowadays it's called tele-conferencing.

The crew whipped up the Peek-a-Vue with a piece of blue paper for the screen and added a couple of knobs. The blue paper gave them the ability to 'key' someone onto the screen. In other words, superimpose them. When someone was on the Peek-a-Vue screen talking with J.P., all the

The evolution of Grandpa Tick-Tock & J.P. Patches.

Clown was really looking at was the blue paper, but at home you could see the person 'keyed' onto the screen. This technique is what they use when weather forecasters are standing in front of big maps that keep changing. They're actually standing in front of a blue or green screen and the map is 'keyed' over it.

Not built to last

A lot of the props for the show were constantly having to be fixed, repainted, glued back together, or simply scrapped and rebuilt. And it's no wonder. The cast and crew played rough.

For a Thanksgiving show they had a bit where J.P. was supposed to burn a turkey (Not Tikey Turkey), and the little oven that Tikey lived in was where he would do the deed. The crew bought some smoke bombs from a theatre supply shop, and like most boys playing with fire, they figured if one smoke bomb makes X amount of smoke, two or three smoke bombs would make it even better! So, naturally, they rigged it with three. When it came time for J.P. to see if the turkey was done they set off the bombs. The explosion blew the back of the plywood oven clean off. Made a darn fine cloud of smoke, too.

PATCHES TRIVIA

J.P. told his viewers that he'd heard of a mysterious beast called a FRPLE and they could help him find it. During the hunt for the Friendly Frple a map was printed up with different places to look, and places to avoid. On the map were three islands, named GNIK (with a silent 'G'), OMOK, and ORIK (Get it?). The kids were told to avoid GNIK AND OMOK. J.P. finally found Ggoorrsstt on Island ORIK, and brought him to live in the secret room under his shack by the city dump.

There is no honor among thieves

The costumes on the show were just as important as any set pieces, but sometimes more than needle and thread patchwork was needed. You can't patch up J.P.'s costume…if it's stolen!

I know, I know, what kind of low-life dirtbag would steal from J.P. and Gertrude? But it happened. In one instance Chris and Bob had just finished a long day of standing on the street corner taking donations for the Children's telethon and

1978, looking tip top in a top hat.

JOIN THE PARADE WITH J.P. PATCHES

PASTE PICTURE HERE

I AM A PATCHES PAL

J. P. Patches

Channel 7 KIRO-TV CBS

were going down to the Edgewater Hotel for dinner. Chris didn't want to take the chance of his J.P. outfit being swiped so he stuck it in his suitcase, put it in his car, drove down to the hotel, had dinner, and drove home. The next morning when he opened the car the suitcase was gone! Without his normal duds Chris had to use his back-up clown clothes until he could get new ones made. The problem was that he didn't have a back-up nose, so he went on the air without his normal clown nose. He just painted his own nose red. Sadly for Chris, no one noticed.

Buttons, buttons, who has the buttons?

Part of the mystique of J.P.'s ever-changing clown coat was the buttons. A constant stream of new buttons was sent in by kids, and at first J.P. thought he'd just keep adding new ones onto the coat, but eventually they became too

PATCHES MEMORIES

Harry Wapler—KIRO Weatherman (1969-02)

"If Chris had an evening appearance somewhere, I'd see him around the station around 5 or 6 o'clock putting on his make-up, and that's when he would sneak onto the news set and wreak his particular brand of havoc. One time in particular, during the news I saw him, in costume, creeping across the floor on his belly, like a soldier crawling under barbed wire. The next thing I know, while I'm doing the weather, I'm reaching down and helping him up. In those days, the numbers and letters we used for showing temperatures and wind speeds were magnetic and you just stuck them onto the weatherboard. Well, J.P.'s standing there next to me and out of the blue he hits my weather-board with his fist, and to my dismay everything fell off the board like an earthquake hit it."

heavy. Plus, the buttons made a racket, clattering around whenever he moved. It was annoying for J.P. and gave the guy in the audio booth fits. From that moment on all new buttons were swapped in on a rotating basis.

That cool carpet with the games on it

One of the more memorable props on J.P.'s set was one that didn't do a darn thing. It just laid there. It was the carpet. But what a carpet! What made

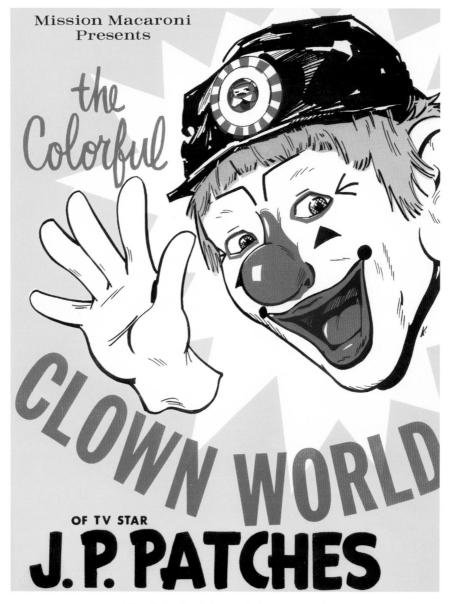

J.P. coloring book from Mission Macaroni.

the magic house's new carpet such a big deal was that it was such a shocking departure from what used to be there. The simple fact is *nothing used to be there*. One day J.P.'s floor was gray, the next, fluorescent green, yellow and orange. It practically screamed at you. And for many Patches Pals who grew up watching the show in black and white for several years (it wasn't until 1977 that even 75% of American homes had color TVs) it was a shock. But a cool one. When you're a kid, anything loud and tasteless is cool.

One Patches Pal, who was raised in a house that was a little slow in making the transition to color television, vividly recalls visiting a friend who had a color TV and seeing, for the first time, the Patches show in color. When he saw that vibrant floor with the games and numbers printed right on the carpet it was like some sort of biblical epiphany. "Yea, and the scales fell from mine eyes and I saw the Patches show for the Technicolor wonder that it truly was."

That carpet was a kid's dream. Chinese checkers, chess, all sorts of games printed right there on the floor for you to play anytime you darn well felt like it. J.P. got the new flooring from the owner of a local carpet company who offered to carpet the shack by the city dump after he noticed the Clown slip a couple of times on the show. Chris agreed to try out the carpet and before long J.P. was waltzing around on the busy, fluorescent green carpet that became a fixture on the show. The carpet maker soon experienced a run on that pattern.

How did J.P. become Mayor of the city dump? On the very first show, Mr. Slick (played by Dick Hawkins) stood on the set, wondering if "Maybe some sucker would come along and buy this dump." That sucker was J.P.. The oily Mr. Slick promised J.P. if he bought the shack he could be Mayor of the whole city dump! A handshake later and the rest is political history.

I love my Patches Pals thiiiiiis much.

How Big Was J.P.?

• • • • • • • • • • • • • •

When sports figures become so popular that they transcend the sport they play they're described as being bigger than the game. Michael Jordan, Tiger Woods, Babe Ruth: even if you didn't watch them play you knew who they were. In the Pacific Northwest, J.P. Patches was bigger than the game. In 1978 he even got his own day! Seattle Mayor Charles Royer commemorated October 14th as J.P. Patches Day. Thousands packed the Seattle Center grounds to honor the Clown.

Recently, at one of J.P.'s public appearances a friend of mine heard a woman point at J.P. and comment to her daughter, "Oh look, a clown!" *A clown?* She might as well have put a red flashing light on her head with a sign that says, 'I'm not from here!' Anyone growing up within shouting distance of Puget Sound knows J.P. Patches on sight and by name. Wear a tee shirt with his smiling mug on the front and it doesn't matter where you go around the Seattle area, you're guaranteed a comment or two.

His demographic appeal was so broad KIRO's advertising sales staff should have named all their children after him in gratitude. His popularity

Where J.P. goes, kids follow.

bridged generations, economic status, and cliques. Every type of kid imaginable watched J.P.: the geeks, the bullies, the popular kids, the invisible kids, all were drawn to the Clown. And the reasons were as varied as the kids. They could relate to J.P.; he frequently got into trouble. They could feel superior to J.P.; he did ridiculous things. They were drawn to him because he wasn't a namby-pamby, goody-two-shoes; J.P. always seemed to be up to something. He wasn't preachy, but lessons were learned. He was never mean, but frequently tried to get the better of others. As a result, those others usually got the better of him.

Young people may be as different as snowflakes, but ask any parent and they'll tell you, a kid is still a kid. And kids loved J.P.

As long-time *Seattle Times* columnist, Erik Lacitis, eloquently points out:

> Some people wonder why J.P. had fans who were punks and dressed all in black clothes and black make-up. I think the reason is that everybody seeks an anchor in their lives. Maybe that anchor doesn't come from your dysfunctional family. Maybe at some moments it comes from J.P., a 100% nice guy, 100% all of the time. He was about having a friend who didn't judge you harshly. He was about that romanticized family in the U.S. of A., in which Moms and Dads don't fight, and don't get divorced, and parents and kids aren't yelling at each

other. Believe it or not, no matter what their street posture was hanging out on the 'Ave' in the U-district, or on Capitol Hill, even the punkiest of punks has that hope, although it might be well hidden.

They gave 'til he hurt

Everyone loved catching a glimpse of J.P. and Gertrude. It was, for many Northwesterners, a celebrity moment: a brush with greatness. In 1965 the Clown and Gertrude stood on a street corner, collecting money for the Children's telethon. Hundreds of cars drove up to make donations, mostly by parents who wanted to give their kids in the backseat a chance to see J.P. and Gertrude in person, even if it was only long enough to drop a dollar in the bucket. By the end of the day they collected over five thousand dollars, mostly in small bills. It was nearly ten percent of the telethon's entire collection. What difference can a couple of clowns make?

The following year while Chris was driving to the telethon, another car ran a stop light and T-boned him. Chris was hospitalized and never made it to the telethon. The telethon didn't reach its goal that year.

The day after the accident the *Seattle Times* ran a large photo of Chris, *not in J.P. make up!*, from when he was being helped into the ambulance, his head bandaged and his arm in a sling. The headline blared, "Hey Kids! This IS J.P. Patches!"

You never saw the Swami of Pastrami in November and December. Bob Newman used the same voice for the Swami and Santa and didn't want anyone to notice, so he had them keep their distance.

Keep those card & letters coming.

Bad idea.

As a result of that headline, the *Times* may have set a company record for cancelled subscriptions.

The accident put Chris in the hospital and kept him off the show for a couple of weeks, but his time off wasn't exactly restful. Word got out about where he was staying and the kid network took it from there. A steady stream of half-pints flocked to the hospital and peered through his window. To top it off, nurses, orderlies and doctors were always asking for his autograph. The get-well cards numbered in the thousands.

Fan mail

During the height of J.P.'s popularity a day didn't go by when he wouldn't receive cards or letters from Patches Pals. Chris still has boxes of them. The cards give thanks, ask questions, or just offer a hello from fans who wanted to reach out to the hero they watched, day after day. A boy writes to thank J.P. for helping him smile while his brother was in Viet Nam. A little girl, newly transplanted to America shares that the Patches show helped her learn English. A father writes to tell Chris that his daughter named her horse 'Patches Pal' and it just won a race at Longacres.

A million letters, a million memories.

The highlight for thousands of children in the Puget Sound area was appearing on J.P.'s show, but running a close second was seeing him at a public appearance. Television was still a relatively new phenomenon in the Sixties so the glamour factor was a lot higher than it is today. For a kid growing up in those times, to see their TV heroes in real life, in color, was a tremendous thrill.

It also could mess with a little kid's reality. Chris remembers one public appearance in Lynnwood where a little girl confronted him and said, "You're not J.P. Patches!" Chris said, "I'm not?" "No," replied the little girl, emphatically, "J.P. Patches is black and white."

When the Clowns showed up you could guarantee a full house.

Patches & his public.

Opening night for Star Wars? Nope, just another J.P. Patches appearance.

When kids meet the clown, time stands still.

J.P. and Gertrude made live appearances at local malls, grocery stores, McDonald's restaurants, you name it. And they did it just about every weekend. In other words, they almost never had a weekend free for twenty-three years straight. Their wives were less than thrilled. Just this year, Bob Newman, after struggling with multiple sclerosis for over two decades finally retired Gertrude from doing public appearances. But Chris still dons J.P.'s make-up and patchwork coat to do three or four public appearances a month, twenty years after he and his sidekick went off the air.

Missed opportunities

The countless public appearances thrilled their fans but they cost Chris and Bob several opportunities.

One such opportunity came when the agency that handled an up and coming restaurant called Chris and asked him if he'd be free to fly to Chicago to audition for the part of the restaurant's new spokesman. The audition was on Saturday and Chris was doing a public appearance at a local McDonald's

Early 60s J.P. & Gertrude.

so he couldn't make it. The next week they called him again, and invited him to audition, but Chris was still booked. He never did find time to audition for what would later become a clown named Ronald McDonald. Incidentally, the man who won the part was none other than, *NBC Today Show* weatherman, Willard Scott.

Back when McDonald's restaurant signs proudly boasted, '*More than one million served*', J.P. and Gertrude were doing public appearances all over town, opening new McDonald's franchises. At the time there were only six or seven McDonald's restaurants in the Seattle area, but J.P.'s commercials and public appearances were so popular the McDonald's people offered to sell Chris one of the restaurants for $40,000! They offered him the one in Ballard at 5400 NW 14th, but Chris grew up in the restaurant business and wasn't interested in diving back into the food service pool. Next time you drive by that McDonald's, just think, it could have been McPatches.

Alaskan pirates

Chris's McDonald's connection wasn't over yet. The man who normally played Ronald McDonald in Washington State had just been sacked, so when the Alaska McDonald's restaurants made a request to have Ronald put in an appearance there wasn't a Ronald to send. The local agency that handled

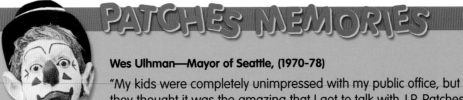

PATCHES MEMORIES

Wes Ulhman—Mayor of Seattle, (1970-78)

"My kids were completely unimpressed with my public office, but they thought it was the amazing that I got to talk with J.P. Patches or Gertrude from time to time. That alone made me a hero in my kid's eyes."

87

PATCHES TRIVIA

Bob Newman has the distinct honor of holding the world record for taking the most pies in the face on live television in a half-hour. In 1972, a representative from Guinness Book of Records showed up to verify that Gertrude took 675 pies in the face. Off camera there was an assembly line of people making whipped cream pies while Gertrude took the brunt of it throughout the show. Over all the years, Newman took hundreds and hundreds of pies in the face. J.P.? Maybe a dozen. Maybe.

Gertrude, suckers, & a woman with outstanding hair.

McDonald's called Chris to see if he'd put on the red afro and striped socks and make a trip up north. Chris finally got his chance to play Ronald. He was invited back six months later to make another Ronald run, and spent the better part of the morning doing radio interviews as Ronald McDonald.

Later that day, when he was in a parade in Fairbanks someone hollered at him, "Hey, J.P. we heard you on the radio. We recognize your voice!" Chris was thinking, "How in heaven's name could someone in Fairbanks recognize my voice?" They either had to be from Seattle or they somehow watched the show. But there was no way they could see the Patches show way up there. Could they? Actually, they could. In the late Sixties Chris started getting fan mail from Alaska, with parents asking J.P. to wish their kids happy birthday on the ICU2TV. This puzzled Chris. He knew KIRO's signal was strong, but it wasn't strong enough to reach Alaska. After a little snooping around Chris discovered an outfit on Capitol Hill was recording Seattle TV shows and sending them to stations in small Alaska towns like Cordova, and St. Petersburg. What they were doing wasn't even remotely legal, but Chris didn't see any up-side to making a fuss about it so he let the pirates continue spreading the Patches show to the Last Frontier. He even got fan mail from someone who was getting tapes of the show sent to them in Guam.

In search of the elusive FRPLE at Woodland Park Zoo.

Audience specific

The popularity of J.P. in Seattle is unquestioned, with legions of Patches Pals throughout every neighborhood. But Gertrude has her own vocal fan base. Generally known as *Gertrude's Gang*, the fans of Miss City Dump are famous for their enthusiastic hero worship. And their diversity. Chris noticed that when he and Bob went down the Seafair parade route there would always be hundreds of people yelling for J.P. and a few for Gertrude (Gertrude disputes this). But every time the parade reached a certain block the cheering ratio would reverse. The crowd went crazy for Gertrude. It turns out it was at that point that the parade passed a gay bar. Must have been the cross-dressing connection.

They should offer hazard pay

The public appearances were always popular but one time things got down right dangerous! It all started when Ggoorrsstt went AWOL. Eventually, J.P. told his viewers Ggoorrsstt was spotted at the Woodland Park Zoo, and asked kids to show up and help her and Ketchikan track down the wiley Frple. The viewers weren't promised anything, no goodie bags, no chance to be on the show, nothing. They were just told to show up with a white band around their arm with the letters O.F.F. (Official Frple Finder). Close to five thousand kids showed up.

Since Bob Newman was playing Ketchikan that day, Jim Clark, one of the show's floor directors, had to climb inside the furry Frple costume. While thousands of kids scoured the zoo grounds with J.P. and Ketch, Jim sat in one of the caged zoo exhibits waiting to be found.

As it turns out, the cage Jim was in was right next to the orangutan cage

PATCHES MEMORIES

Bill McLain—Alias, 'Brakeman Bill' on KTNT/KSTW (1955-75)

"When I would share the bill with J.P. and Gertrude at public appearances, I must confess that I laughed as hard as the people in the audience. They were consummate comedians. I remember that, at one time, J.P., Stan Boreson, Captain Puget, and I all had the same personal appearance manager. A real character named Whitey, who wore a derby and smoked cheap cigars. Whitey finally abandoned us to work as the advance man for Ringling Brothers Circus. How appropriate."

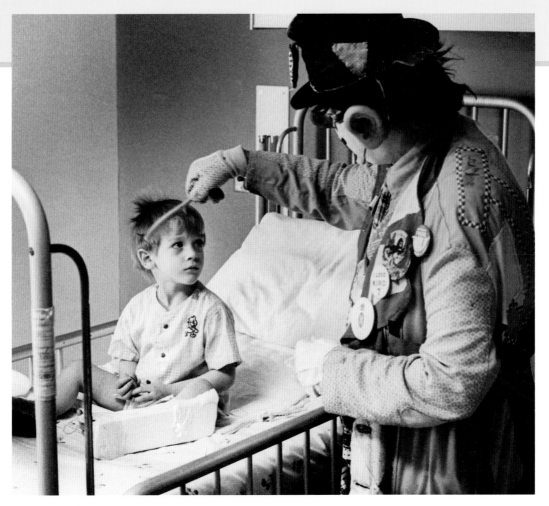

J.P. at Children's Hospital.

and apparently these simians had never seen a Frple, up close before. They reacted like most apes react to something they're not familiar with, they threw things. Poor Jim was pelted with anything the orangutans could get their mitts on.

By the time the kids found Ggoorrsstt they were swarming. When Jim got out of the cage the kids were on him like locust. It was like Elvis in fur. He had to climb on top of a station wagon before the kids tore his antennae and fur off. Ah, the price of fame.

Children's hospital

J.P.'s connection with children was legendary. Over the years he made countless trips to Children's Hospital to visit kids who didn't have a lot to smile about. He never patronized them, never treated them any differently than a healthy child. And they loved him for it.

In 1978, Chris was finally recognized for his years of spreading cheer. A

J.P. was asked to introduce the grunge band Soundgarden when they performed their homecoming concert in Seattle. He wasn't familiar with who they were (generational difference) but agreed because they were fans. When he stepped out on stage to the roar of thousands of Soundgarden fans, J.P. quipped, "What the hell am I doing here?" It was the only time J.P. ever cursed in front of his fans.

77-year old Patches Pal named Dorothy Bettcher gave $50,000 to the Children's Orthopedic Hospital in J.P.'s name so they could build a play area for visiting brothers and sisters of kids in the hospital. It was the first time a part of the hospital was named for someone other than a physician, hospital guild member, donor, or person associated in some regard with the institution. When the hospital announced the gift, live, on J.P.'s

Turn your head & cough!

show, it was probably one of the only times in Patches' history that the Clown was left speechless on his own show. Unfortunately, just a few years ago the J.P. Patches play area was removed. A victim of the hospital's remodeling.

The people have spoken

If there was ever any doubt about the popularity of the Clown the *Seattle Times* ended it with a poll it conducted in October, 2001. The paper asked readers to help compile a list of the 150 most influential people in Seattle's history. On this list of people who shaped Seattle — a list that includes Bill Gates, Jimi Hendrix, Dexter Horton, Warren Magnuson and Chief Seattle himself — are J.P. Patches and Gertrude.

Duration

From start to finish, The *J.P. Patches Show* aired from 1958-1981. When the Clown finally bowed out, the show held the record for the longest running local children's program in America. At its peak Patches aired weekday mornings at 7:30, afternoons at 5:00 and Saturday mornings at 7:30. It wasn't until 1973 that the afternoon show was pulled, and on Friday, December 29th, 1978, the morning show was also cancelled. Temporarily.

At the height of his popularity J.P. attracted 100,000 viewers a day. By the time they pulled the plug the latest ratings indicated that his audience had dwindled to 10,000. In spite of the low viewership, when the announcement was made that the weekday morning show was being scratched, the station was flooded with angry calls and letters. How angry? Think medieval townfolk wielding pitchforks and torches. One-year later J.P.'s weekday show was back on the

First season show: 1958

Pat O'Day—KJR AM Radio DJ/Program director/General Manager/Voice of the Hydro Races

"Chris is the consummate performer. With all the grease paint and the costume he still went out every time and never disappointed. He always signed the autograph, always had the great attitude. The man is at the top of the mountain when it comes to dedication."

air, but when kids tuned in they found that the Clown had been relocated from the city dump to city hall, and some of the magic seemed to have been lost in the move. On September 21st, 1981, the *J.P. Patches Show* went off the air permanently.

Chris and Bob stuck around KIRO for a few more years before retiring, but that didn't seem to slow the demand for J.P. and Gertrude. They were still just as busy as ever doing personal appearances, except now many of the Patches Pals for whom they were performing were grown ups looking for one more chance to meet their slapstick idols, face to face.

15th anniversary with Bill Mudge, Paul Bishop, Stan Borenson, and Don McCune.

A fan of the show owned a racehorse and named it Patches Pal. It raced at Longacres.

When J.P. went on the air in Seattle...

✳ Dwight Eisenhower was President.

✳ Nikita Khrushchev became Premier of the USSR.

✳ Charles deGaulle became Premier of France.

✳ The first U.S. satellite was launched (The Explorer).

✳ NASA was formed.

✳ Alaska became the 49th state.

✳ The first credit cards appeared (American Express).

✳ Jimmy Hoffa became head of the Teamsters Union.

✳ Michelle Pfeiffer, Alec Baldwin, Drew Carey, Sharon Stone, Michael Jackson and Madonna were born.

✳ *Gunsmoke* was the most popular TV show in America.

✳ Gigi won the Academy Award for best picture.

✳ On the radio people were listening to *At the Hop*, by Danny and the Juniors, *Tequila*, by the Champs, and *The Purple People Eater*, by Sheb Wooley.

✳ The Hula-Hoop and the Barbie Doll were invented.

✳ The life expectancy was 69.6 years.

✳ Minimum wage was $1.

✳ Average income was $4,650.

✳ A new car was $2,155.

✳ A new house was $11,975.

✳ A loaf of bread was 19 cents.

✳ A gallon of milk was $1.01.

✳ A gallon of gas was 24 cents.

When J.P. went off the air...

* MTV went on the air.

* There were assassination attempts on President Reagan and Pope John Paul II.

* American Hostages in Iran were released after 444 days.

* Prince Charles and Lady Diana Spencer were married.

* The PC was launched by IBM.

* The first reusable spacecraft, the space shuttle Columbia, was also launched.

* Sandra Day O'Conner became the first woman elected to the Supreme Court.

* A Major League Baseball strike split the season into two halves.

* *Raiders of the Lost Ark* lost the Academy Award for best picture to *Chariots of Fire*.

* Walter Cronkite retired.

* Life expectancy was 73.2 years.

* On the radio people were listening to *Bette Davis Eyes*, by Kim Carnes, *Physical*, by Olivia Newton-John, and *Endless Love*, by Diana Ross and Lionel Richie.

* Average income was $11,661.

* A new car was $5,743.

* A new house was $96,240.

* A loaf of bread was 54 cents.

* A gallon of milk was $1.69.

Charlie Can-Do
(Bob Newman)

Officer Paddy
Wagon
(Bob Newman)

Characters

· · · · · · · · · · · · · ·

(All characters played by Bob Newman unless otherwise noted)

✳ *Mr. X.R. Cize*—J.P.'s fitness guru. He had a short life on the show

✳ *Howard Huge*—Hardly worth mentioning. Only made one appearance

✳ *Andy Granitebelly*—Named after the race car driver, Andy Granatelli. You never saw Andy, only heard him. He stayed outside the window in the back of the set. You could see a bit of his car back there. He made very, very few appearances.

✳ *Charlie Can-Do*—The Confucius spewing Chinese detective. After a few years Charlie was dumped in the name of political correctness.

✳ *Chief MoonRay*—The Native American you never saw, only heard. He too was politically corrected off the show.

✳ *Zenobia*—(gasp)—The evil witch, ally of Boris S. Wart

✳ *Paddy Wagon*—The Irish cop. Originally played by Bill Gerald, then later, Bob Newman.

✳ *Leroy Frump*—Resident handyman with the IQ of a lugwrench. He showed up by climbing a ladder through a hole that J.P. would unfold and lay on the floor.

✳ *Dingbatman*—Superhero with cool theme song and cardboard wings. Always circling above the skies of Seattle to protect the Lake Washington Bridges, the Ballard Bridge and the Space Needle from being blown up by Boris.

✳ *Sam Gefeltefish*—J.P.'s mythical director. Okay, not too mythical. He actually showed up on the show, in person a couple of times. Usually you just heard his indecipherable, high-speed voice on the phone. Played by real show director, Joe Towey.

The Rivoli, a popular burlesque club in downtown Seattle, starred a stripper who thought she'd cash in on J.P.'s popularity. She began billing herself as 'J.P.-(rhymes with Patches, starts with Sn)'. The people at KIRO were not amused.

* *Boris S. Wart*—Second Meanest Man in the World and J.P.'s nemesis. If a kid ever asked them who was the first meanest man, J.P. would tell them, "I think you know who it is," and the kid would always say something like, "Yea, my principal."

* *Miss Smith*—Delivery Service Woman, always played *Is it a hit* (ding) *or a miss?* (clunk) with J.P.. Miss Smith was based on a female taxi driver that Chris and Bob would always see when they were outside on the street corner collecting money for the Children's telethon.

Boris S. Wart

Mr. X.R. Cize

✳ *Ketchikan*—The Animal Man. Started and stopped his own theme music by tapping the top of his pith helmet. The original animal man was named Uncle Jack, played by Jack Armstrong. When Jack left, Bob Newman took the role and came up with Ketchikan Cal, purveyor of the Bongo Congo Kennels.

✳ *Ggoorrsstt*—The Friendly Frple who eats Frple Fodder on Fridays from Farmer Fred in Fife or Farmer Frank in Ferndale. Eats through his armpits. The Frple was named after the small town outside of Bremerton.

✳ *Swami of Pastrami*—Local mystic with a big white beard, turban and crystal ball whose voice sounded suspiciously like Santa's.

✳ *Sturdley the Bookworm*—The resident green worm who lived in the crooked bookshelf in the back left corner of the set. Sturdley had a voracious appetite for books, which he would chew up the minute J.P. gave him some. Jack Armstrong, Buzz Anderson (a floor director), Bill Gerald and Bob Newman, all did the voice of Sturdley.

The Swami of Pastrami

* *Morgan the Frog*—The green puppet, made by Gloria Hillard, would usually show up at J.P.'s door for no reason whatsoever. His croaky voice was Bob Newman inhaling when he spoke.

* *Deepen Hock*—Sounding like W.C. Fields, Deepen was always trying to borrow something from J.P. Bill Gerald played Deepen, but the character didn't last long.

* *Grandma, Grandpa Patches*—Originally played by Craig Shreeve, who later took his acting chops to Hollywood, winning roles in *General Hospital, Falcon Crest, Starsky & Hutch, Close Encounters of the Third Kind* and *Ice Station Zebra*, to name a few. When Craig left Chris donned the spectacles of the elder clowns.

* *Professor Wiener Von Brrrrown*—The Wonder from Cape Blunder was a take-off on NASA Saturn rocket engineer Professor Wernher von Braun. The Professor was played by Bill Gerald and would frequently host the show if J.P. was on vacation in Clown Town, or unable to perform.

PATCHES MEMORIES

Ed Hume—Northwest Gardener extrordinaire

"When J.P. and I were both making an appearance at the Tacoma Film Festival, J.P. was supposed to introduce the Mayor of Tacoma who had a speech prepared to kick off the festival. Well, J.P. stole all of his notes so the Mayor had to do what all politicians hate to do — he had to wing it."

Super Clown

✳ *Mal Content*— General handyman and precursor to Leroy Frump. Played by Joe Towey.

✳ *I.M Raggs*—J.P.'s evil twin brother. Played by Joe Towey.

✳ *Super Clown*—Orphaned son from the planet Kronkton. Never seen in the company of J.P. Patches. Hmmmmm. Played by Chris Wedes.

✳ *Mr. Slick*—The Con Man who sold J.P. the shack by the city dump. Slick was played by Dick Hawkins.

✳ *The Wizard of Gizzard*—Paul Bishop played the Wizard of Gizzard, who preceded the Swami of Pastrami. The Wizard acted as a preacher to marry Gertrude and I.M. Raggs.

✳ *Sheriff Shot Badly*—A klutzy John Wayne, he kept tripping over his own feet. Played by Don Einarson, the Sheriff actually had his own show on KIRO for 26 weeks. Don was the station announcer before Hal Willard (Mr. Announcer Man).

✳ *Mike Boom*— The hanging boom microphone used on the show. Sometimes the mike would drop into frame, so J.P. simply gave it a name and turned it into another character on the show.

Leroy Frump snaps his own suspenders for a change.

OFFICIAL CLOWN BALLOT
Mayor of Pugetopolis

SELECT ONE

BORIS S. WORT
Dragon Party

Currently second meanest man in the world. If elected he promises to be number one. Campaign slogan **"WIN WITH WORT!"** Reommended by Morris Wort, Doris Wort & Horace Wort.

☐ **I vote Boris S. Wort**
Check Here

J.P. PATCHES
Turkey Party

Currently Mayor of City Dump. Promises to continue entertaining, informing and serving the community if elected. **"PUT A REAL CLOWN IN OFFICE."** Recommended by **everyone**, except Boris, Doris & Horace Wort.

☐ **I vote J.P.Patches**
Check Here

Theme Songs

* * * * * * * * * * * * * *

❋ Opening Theme: (What J.P woke up to) Spike Jones' *Dance of the Hours*

❋ Closing Theme: Beginning in the mid-Sixties, after pouring over count-less records Chris and Duane settled on the *Carroll Baker-a-Go-Go* from the movie *Harlow*, for the closing theme. Neil Hefti, who wrote the song also wrote the theme song for *Batman* and *The Odd Couple*. Dingbatman's theme song was also a Neil Hefti song.

❋ Ketchikan's theme song: *Our Director*, by Frederick Ellsworth Bigelow.

❋ Mr. Announcer Man's theme song: *In the Mood*, sometimes the standard version, sometimes the Ray Stevens' Hen House Five Plus Two version, complete with chickens clucking in tune.

❋ Ooga Chugga Singers: (The music you heard when J.P. opened the secret room) *Hooked on a Feeling*, by Blue Swede.

❋ I'd rather be a Patches Pal: Sung to the tune of *I'd Like to Teach the World to Sing (In Perfect Harmony)*. The original song was made popular in 1972 by The New Seekers, then made even more popular by being used in the infamous hillside singers Coca-Cola commercial where they sang, 'I'd like to buy the world a Coke'.

Here are the actual lyrics to the Patches version.

> *I'd rather be a Patches Pal than a Boris Buddy mean,*
> *I'll mind my mom, I'll mind my dad and keep my room so clean.*
> *I'll do the things upon the list, I'll check them one by one,*
> *I'd rather be a Patches Pal 'cuz they have all the fun.*
> *I'm a Patches Pal, all day long,*
> *'Cuz a Patches Pal knows right from wrong.*

Jayne Meadows & Steve Allen

Famous Guests

* * * * * * * * * * * * *

❋ *Jesse Owen*—Olympic gold medallist, and the only person Chris ever asked for an autograph. Minutes later it was stolen.

❋ *Steve Allen and Jayne Meadows*—Host of the *Tonight Show*/his wife. Steve was a great guest. He even knocked over a display rack of potato chips right before a live commercial.

❋ *Burt Ward*—Robin of *Batman and Robin* fame

❋ *Clayton Moore*—The Lone Ranger, appeared with Chris on *Joe the Cook's Popcorn Party*.

❋ *Tiny Tim*—*Laugh-In* regular, ukulele playing goofball famous for playing *Tiptoe Through the Tulips*. This was at the height of Tiny Tim's popularity. It was the only time they ever locked the studio doors to prevent people from getting in. Even then, a mob of people clustered around every window that looked down on the studio.

❋ *Colonel Harlan Sanders*—Kentucky Fried Chicken magnate, before they changed the name to KFC ('Fried' is a bad word in marketing). The Colonel went off, on camera, about how badly the local franchises were preparing his secret recipe. Off camera, the Colonel's PR guys pulled their hair out.

❋ *Debbie Reynolds*—Hollywood leading lady and songbird, most notable for her starring role in *Singin' in the Rain*.

❋ *Beverly Garland*—Actress most recognized from the television show, *My 3 Sons*. She appeared on the Patches show without warning, dressed up as Gertrude. The night before Chris was doing his fake waiter routine at her hotel and really had her believing he was an utterly incompetent restaurant employee. Beverly, showing up out of the blue on his show was classy revenge.

The Colonel meets the Clown.

✳ *Slim Pickens*—Famous 'Aw-shucks' character actor from films like *Dr. Strangelove* and *Blazing Saddles*, Pickens could cuss like a drunken sailor. And he did, right up 'til the moment the camera tally-lights came on.

✳ *Other notable guests*—Dixie Lee Ray (Governor of Washington), Merrilee Rush (*Angel of the Morning*), Jacques Cousteau, Al Capp (Cartoonist of *Lil' Abner*), The Harlem Globetrotters, Danny Thomas, Jack LaLane.

Clayton Moore — The Lone Ranger

The first time Ketchikan bought an animal onto the show, J.P. asked him what the animal's name was and Ketch threw out the first name that came to mind. From that point on, all the animals Ketchikan brought onto the show were named 'Fred'. Coincidentally, six months later, all the animals that showed up on the Red Skelton show were also named 'Fred'.

Bill McLain (a.k.a. — Brakeman Bill)

Other Notable Northwest TV Personalities

Bill McLain (Brakeman Bill)

Brakeman Bill and his sidekick puppet, 'Crazy Donkey', graced Northwest airwaves from 1955-1975, on KTNT/KSTW. Needing a kid's show, the brain trust at channel 11 decided to copy a popular Los Angeles television program (*Engineer Bill*). Now all they needed was someone to play the Engineer. They found their host in a gentleman named Dave Richardson, but two days before the show went on the air Dave was diagnosed with polio. In stepped Bill McLain. At the time Bill was the station's sports director, part-time booth announcer, part-time cameraman, part-time just about everything. They fitted him with some overalls, gave him a railroad hat and pointed him toward the set. Bill really didn't have a clue as to what he was supposed to do but his boss told him, "It's simple, introduce some cartoons, talk to the kids in the audience, and if you run out of things to say, run the trains. Heck, if all else fails, draw a funny cartoon." Before long Brakeman Bill was a smash success!

Bill's trusty on-air puppet partner was the wisecracking 'Crazy Donkey'. Sewn together by a station secretary, and voiced by ex-disc jockey Warren Reed, Crazy Donkey played Lewis to Brakeman Bill's Martin. He joked around, got into trouble and became the object lesson for children of what NOT to do.

(For more information see the Brakeman Bill website — www.brakemanbill.com)

Stan Borenson, Brakeman Bill, J.P., Capt. Puget.

Courtesy of Museum of History and Industry

Gertrude's pet pigs, which you heard but never saw, were named Fred and Ethel, after the neighbors of Lucy and Ricky Ricardo on I Love Lucy.

Stan Boreson

The 'King of Scandinavian Humor', Stan Boreson appeared for eighteen years on several Seattle television shows, including his longest running, *KING's Klubhouse* on channel 5. Stan made a name for himself on local TV by capitalizing on Seattle's large Scandinavian population. Armed with his accordion, Stan began transforming popular American songs into humorous Norwegian and Swedish versions. On *KING's Klubhouse*, you would always find Stan singing along with his molasses-reflexed dog, No-Mo. Anyone growing up in the Puget Sound area became familiar with

Stan Boreson

Captain Puget

Stan's secret password to get into the *KING Klubhouse*: Zero Dockus Mucho Crockus Halabuluzabub.

(For more information see the Stan Boreson website — www.stanboreson.com)

Don McCune (Captain Puget)

In 1957, Don McCune took the helm of KOMO-TV's *Captain Puget Show*. The laid-back, pipe smoking Captain skippered the popular children's program for nine years. Singing sea chanteys and songs about the Northwest, Don also took kids on filmed adventures around Puget Sound. It was these adventures that eventually led to Don's other hugely popular KOMO-TV show, *Exploration Northwest*, which ran from 1960-1981.

True Northwesterners will remember Don's first mate for the first two seasons of the Captain Puget show was none other than the King of Keeping Clam, Ivar Haglund.

(For more information see the Don McCune website — www.donmccunelibrary.com)

Ruth Prins (Wunda Wunda)

"Wunda Wunda is my name; boys and girls we're glad you came." With these lyrics Northwest pre-schoolers were introduced to a magical puppet, come to life, Wunda Wunda. Weekday mornings at 8:30, the purple and gold dressed Wunda Wunda told stories, sang songs and entertained children for many years on KING-TV. Ruth Prins was the woman behind Wunda. Between her and the show's musical accompaniment (the off-stage organist, Elliot Brown) Wunda Wunda shared a wide-eyed innocence with her audience from 1953 to 1972. Ms. Prins also hosted channel 5's *Teladventure Tales* and the nationally watched *Compass Rose*.

Courtesy of Museum of History and Industry

Wunda Wunda

Joe Towey (The Count)

The man calling the shots in the control booth, directing the *J.P. Patches Show* for twenty years, was Joe Towey (or, as Mr. Announcer Man called him, Joseephus, Josiiiiiias Towey). But Joe had an alter ego with which local viewers were much more familiar. Joe was also Seattle's resident vampire, The Count. As host of KIRO-TV's Friday late-night, time-slot winning *Nightmare Theater*, Joe, with his chalky face, pointy fangs and psychotic laugh, rose from his coffin and usually provided more entertainment than the movie he was introducing. Ironically, years before he got into the TV business Joe was a grave salesman.

The Count

Erik Lacitis—Seattle Times columnist (1973-present)

"Back in 1978, as a young columnist for the Seattle Times I went to interview J.P when the show was on its end run. What struck me when I met him in person was… what a nice guy he was. He straddled the world of television executives who dictated to him about the commercials, the cartoons and everything else, and the world of his audience…all those kids. He always managed to be on the side of the kids. The J.P. I had watched on TV when I was young actually was that way in real life: an aw-shucks kind of person, devoid of pretense or even an inkling of meanness."

Other terrific NW websites to check out…

www.jppatches.com
(The official Patches website)

www.callihan.com
(A Seattle Lexicon.
Everything you could ever
want to know about the Northwest
and its pop-culture)

And while we're talking about computers…

Pick up the *J.P. Patches Desktop Set for Windows* (City Dump Productions). Download many of the sounds and images from the show onto your computer. Receive e-mails to the sound of the ICU2TV set. Watch J.P. ride his magic carpet across your screen! A must for the true Patches Pal.

J.P. sort of made an appearance on an episode of the animated TV series, The Simpsons. On 'Radio Bart' (3rd season, episode 8F-11), Krusty the Clown scrolls birthday greetings on the screen, ala the ICU2TV. Among the list of names that scroll down at hyper speed is J.P. Patches. Of course, Krusty charged everyone $8 for the service.

The Clown. The Crew.

For additional copies...

Use the form below to order additional copies of
J.P. Patches — A Northwest Icon or contact Peanut Butter
Publishing at (206) 860-4900.

ORDER FORM

J.P. Patches — A Northwest Icon

Name_____

Address_____

City _____ State _____ Zip _____

Phone _____

Please send me _____ books @ $18.95/book $ _____
Shipping and Handling $ 5.00
Washington State Residents add 8.8% Sales Tax $ _____
                                    Total enclosed $ _____

Please make checks payable to Peanut Butter Publishing

Mail to:

Peanut Butter Publishing
2207 Fairview Avenue East, Houseboat Number Four
Seattle, Washington 98102

For additional information:

(206) 860-4900